Mother's RECIPES

A Contemporary Collection of Family Treasures

By Sheryn R. Jones and Barbara C. Jones

cookbook resources

Dedication

This cookbook is dedicated to family and the mothers who preserve it and make it grow stronger by preparing meals which nourish the soul as well as the body.

Additional copies of this cookbook may be obtained by sending $16.95 plus $3.50 for postage and handling to the address below.

First Printing May 2000
20,000 copies

Copyright © 2000, Cookbook Resources,
Highland Village, Texas.

ISBN: 0-9677932-0-3

Edited, Designed, Published and Manufactured in the
United States of America by
Cookbook Resources, LLC
541 Doubletree Drive
Highland Village, Texas 75077
972.317.0245
www.cookbookresources.com

Introduction

I don't remember taking my lunch to school, ever. And I never ate in the school cafeteria, not in 12 years of elementary, junior high and high school. Everyday Mother picked us up at school and drove us home to have the lunch she cooked. My brother could always tell what we were having to eat by how she smelled. It was another time and world away from now and it's how I grew up and how I remember homecooked meals.

I remember summers at the lake, when early every Saturday morning, Mother would fry at least 2 or 3 chickens to eat for lunch out on the islands. By noonish, she'd call, "Lunch time. Out of the water. We've got Southern Fried Chicken." Somehow, she knew that was the only thing that would get us out of the water. And while we were reaching for the chicken, she'd put a gooey glob of Sea and Ski on our noses and cheeks because "You're getting too much sun. We have to take care of your nose so you won't look old when you're old." We let her do it because we were busy with the fried chicken.

On my birthday every year in November just about Thanksgiving, she makes pumpkin pies for me instead of cakes. Her Birthday Pumpkin Chiffon Pie (254) is special enough for anyone's birthday, her fried okra makes a Texan slap his knee, her Green Bean Supreme (151), Light and Crispy Waffles (62), Crunchy Bread Sticks (45), Creamy Lemon Pie (256), Apricot Cobbler (262), Cornbread Dressing (187), Scalloped Potatoes (176), Sweet Potato Casserole (177), you know I could write a book about my favorites.

Everyone has his or her favorites at Mother's house. My Dad had more favorites than anyone, my brother has his, so does my sister-in-law, their two kids, my cousin and her ex-husbands, my other cousin, his wife and their two kids and their kids' two kids, all her friends, everyone in the bridge club, every newcomer in town, every new preacher or choir member in our church, every Library Board member for the past who knows how many years, every person who's been at the Cancer Luncheon for the past "x" number of years, every person who buys her cakes, breads, cookies, jellies and casseroles at the

Library Board fundraisers and anybody who's ever been sick or had a death in the family for the last 50 years in my little hometown. Just about everybody in town has their favorites.

She has a way of making people feel special. Maybe it's because she goes to a lot of trouble. There aren't many people who can go to a lot of trouble for other people anymore, but she thinks it's worth the time and effort. She cooks dishes in advance so she can enjoy her family and her guests while they're enjoying the meals or the good bites of whatever is their good fortune. She appears to do it all effortlessly with no trouble and with just one goal in mind, hoping others enjoy themselves.

I don't know how she cooked all those meals for breakfast, lunch and dinner and made all the holidays extra nice because of the food she prepared, but each dish and each meal was important.

There was no MacDonald's, no pizza delivery, no pizza for that matter and no take-out. The Dairy Queen was on the drag, but we only got cokes and ice cream on dates. The Root Beer stand had frozen mugs with great, icy cold root beers, the best in the world, but we didn't eat anything there. You could get burgers at the bowling alley and other food at Ben's Restaurant, but that was about it in our little hometown. Homecooked meals were a necessity and she made them good, really good, and I remember them all.

Mother's heart is on a serving dish and her love and caring is in every whip and stir of every recipe. She shows her love for each of us and for so many others through the food she prepares. I hope we all see it clearly and understand it for what it is, in its purest form and simplest denomination . . . the love of one person expressing how special another person is.

She thinks it's important to remember our favorite recipes. She thinks it's important to show us we're special. I think she's special and I think her recipes are special. I hope you too will enjoy them for your lifetime and know the love and caring for making a favorite recipe for someone special.

Sheryn R. Jones
Editor

4

PATI BANNISTER

Cover: *Puddings and Pies* **by Pati Bannister**

*I*t is an honor for Cookbook Resources to feature a painting by Pati Bannister on the cover of *Mother's Recipes*. Her talent goes beyond ordinary concepts and is extremely rare. In her work one finds the invitation to involvement and participation, making the viewer see, feel, and remember.

Speaking in her soft British accent, Pati Bannister prefers talking about her pets rather than the talent that has made her an American legend. Despite the fact that her paintings sell for as much as $60,000, Pati remains untouched by her success. She is shy and a trifle bewildered by her status as one of America's leading artists.

Listed in Who's Who in American Art and featured in numerous art magazines, Pati Bannister paints originals and offers limited edition prints to collectors around the world through New Masters Publishing. Her art is peopled by delicate young women and girls set against romantically imaginative backgrounds.

She can't remember being particularly encouraged in art as a very young child, but then, most of her childhood memories are centered on World War II. "I was born in Highgate, overlooking London in 1929," she relates, "so I was just nine when the War broke out. My mother sent me to the country, unfortunately the southeast coast, so for a while, I was in the middle of The Battle of Britain. Later, I returned to London— just in time for the Blitz. We children, as a diversion, would see who could pick up the most pieces of shrapnel."

Pati made sketches during her young life, working as an illustrator for the prestigious Riding magazine at the age of thirteen, and ultimately working as an animator for J. Arthur Rank, the moviemaker. "It was a lot like Disney, I guess, but probably not as sophisticated. I spent a great deal of time working on detail, composition, and color mixing," Pati says.

By the age of 22, Pati wanted to travel and came to America

as a governess to a family in Fairfield, Connecticut. She continued to sketch, but moved to Miami to work for Southern Airlines as a stewardess so she could travel more. There Glynn Bannister "was hooked once I saw that pretty girl and heard that English accent," he admitted.

In 1958, the Bannisters moved to New Orleans because it seemed a good place for Pati to begin a serious career as an artist. "Glynn helped me a lot, had a wonderful business sense and adapted his business experience to the art business extremely well." Her work quickly became very popular and the Bannisters opened their first, and then a second, gallery in the French Quarter.

Pati now paints in a glassed studio where wild azaleas bloom, birds feed, and squirrels play just outside her window in the provacy of wooded acres on the Mississippi coast.

Pati is an excellent cook and grows herbs and tomatoes in her garden. The remainder of her garden is planted with flowers. Pati's love of flowers is apparent in her paintings. The paintings she now produces of young women and girls feature flowers that seem to bloom on the canvas. Her work has been labeled "magic realism" because of the moods portrayed in her incredibly detailed work.

Pati continues to be intrigued by accurately capturing the transitory quality of light and the moods created by various types of light. She is also very interested in textures of materials—both natural and manmade. And, she says, she continues to be drawn to the harmonies and subtleties of colors and shapes. The subject usually dictates the medium I use. Most of my works are in acrylic or oil. Although I find pastels and watercolors fun and exciting to do, egg tempera is really my favorite."

Pati Bannister captures the moment and mood through her creation of a special world within each painting. In all cases, however, there is a consistency of vision where flowers in full bloom, richly textured fabrics, the sheen of oriental porcelains or the natural beauty of a sunlit landscape, suggest the importance of and need for beauty in the real world.

Here is where Pati Bannister succeeds where few others do. She identifies, selects, elevates and captures beauty in the world in various and magical ways. This is her ultimate gift and the promise of her amazing art.

Barbara C. Jones

(Mother)

*M*other's Recipes are those of my Mother, Barbara C. Jones. This cookbook is meant in some small way to be a tribute to her and to the love and caring she has shown for her family and her friends through the food she has prepared. She is a special person who has given her time and love to make others feel special.

Her recipes are not complicated or ostentatious, but basic with a flair for unique combinations of ingredients that make them different. She has a terrific gift for making old favorites even better by adding a few new ingredients and even improving on the latest recipes that go around. The time you spend with her and this cookbook will be well worth it.

She was born in a small west Texas town and lost her mother at the age of 12. I think from that time on, she thought about being a mother and all the things she could do and would do for her family. She has done that and more and lives as a shining example for us all.

She married my Dad right after World War II and helped him through dental school. From there they started their life and family in a small north Texas town where they've spent their lives raising kids, volunteering in the community, working in the church and making many, many friends.

She's been active in the Public Library for more than 35 years, serving as its president three times and spearheading the construction of a modern facility. She's played the organ at her church for almost 50 years, served in the Cancer Society for more than 10 years and has done extensive volunteer work. She started her own cookbook distribution business 20 years ago. She got her college degree the same year I finished mine and her grade point was higher.

She's a contemporary lady with traditional values and a heart of gold. She does more than anyone I know and she does everything well. Her example is a difficult one to follow, but one that deserves respect and love.

Contents

DON'T RUIN YOUR APPETTITE.

RISE AND SHINE.

DONT TALK WITH YOUR MOUTH FULL.

Dont be sassy.

Eat your vegetables.

Mind your manners.

Say please and thank you.

Don't ruin your appettite.

Stuffed Banana Peppers

20 banana peppers
1 (7 ounce) can white meat tuna, well drained, mashed
1 egg, boiled and mashed
1 tablespoons minced onion
¼ cup chopped dill pickle
⅓ cup mayonnaise
1 teaspoon prepared mustard
½ teaspoon Creole seasoning
½ teaspoon seasoned pepper

Slice peppers in half lengthwise and take the seeds out. Combine and mix tuna, egg, onion, pickle, mayonnaise, mustard and seasoning. Fill pepper halves and refrigerate until ready to serve.

Chili Cheese Log

1 (8 ounce) package cream cheese, softened
2 cups shredded Cheddar cheese, softened
2 tablespoons mayonnaise
1 tablespoon lemon juice
½ teaspoon garlic powder
½ cup finely chopped pecans
1 teaspoon chili powder
1 teaspoon paprika

In mixing bowl, combine cheeses, mayonnaise, lemon juice and garlic powder. Beat with mixer until well blended. Stir in pecans. Shape into roll about 1½ inches in diameter. Mix together the chili powder and paprika and sprinkle roll with mixture. Roll up cheese log in wax paper and refrigerate. Serve with crackers.

Cheese Puffs

2 cups sharp Cheddar cheese, shredded
1 stick margarine, very soft
½ teaspoon salt
1 teaspoon paprika
½ teaspoon garlic powder
1 cup flour
48 green stuffed olives

In a large mixing bowl, mix cheese and margarine. Stir in dry ingredients and mix well. Wrap a teaspoon of mixture around each olive and place on cookie sheet. Bake at 375 degrees for 15 to 16 minutes.

Shrimp and Cheese Appetizers

1 pound cooked chopped shrimp
4 green onions, chopped, tops too
½ cup mayonnaise
1 cup grated Monterey Jack cheese
½ teaspoon instant chicken bouillon
1 tablespoon chopped pimentos
1 teaspoon Beau Monde seasoning
1 teaspoon dill weed
1 package English muffins

Combine all ingredients except muffins. Mix well. Spread on tops and bottoms of the split muffins and bake at 400 degrees for about 10 minutes or until bubbly. Slice in quarters and serve hot.

Party Sausages

1 cup catsup
1 cup plum jelly
1 tablespoon lemon juice
4 tablespoons prepared mustard
2 (15 ounce) packages tiny smoked sausages

In a saucepan, combine all ingredients except sausages and heat; mix well. Add sausages and simmer for 15 minutes. Serve with cocktail toothpicks. You can substitute the smoked sausages for sliced wieners.

Spinach and Cheese Squares

½ stick margarine
1 cup flour
3 eggs
1 cup milk
1 teaspoon salt
1 teaspoon baking powder
1 teaspoon dry mustard
1 (10 ounce) package frozen spinach, thawed, drained and squeezed dry
8 ounces shredded mozzarella cheese
8 ounces shredded Cheddar cheese

Melt margarine in a 9 x 13 inch baking dish in the oven. In large mixing bowl, combine flour, eggs, milk, salt, baking powder and mustard. Mix well. Add spinach and cheeses, pour into pan. Bake at 350 degrees for 30 minutes. When set, cut into squares and serve warm. Can be reheated.

Spinach Crab Balls

1 tablespoon margarine
1 onion, minced
2 (10 ounce) packages frozen chopped spinach, thawed,
well drained and patted dry
4 eggs
2 tablespoons flour
4 slices bacon, cooked and crumbled
1 stick margarine, softened
1 (7½ ounce) can crabmeat, drained and flaked
2 cups seasoned stuffing crumbled
¼ teaspoon pepper
½ teaspoon salt
½ teaspoon dill weed
¼ teaspoon garlic powder

Melt margarine in skillet. Stir in onion and sauté. Mix thoroughly with remaining ingredients. Form into ½ inch balls and place on baking sheet. Bake at 325 degrees for 15 minutes. Serve warm. These can be served plain or with Sweet and Hot Mustard on page 238.

If you want to make ahead and bake when you're ready
to serve — just freeze spinach balls on the baking sheet;
then remove to a baggie to store frozen.

Smoked Salmon Log

1 (15 ounce) can red salmon
1 (8 ounce) package cream cheese, softened
1 tablespoon lemon juice
2 tablespoons grated onion
¼ teaspoon salt
¼ teaspoon liquid smoke
6 tablespoons very finely crushed crackers
1 cup very finely chopped pecans
3 tablespoons minced fresh parsley

Drain salmon; remove skin and bones; flake salmon with fork. In mixer bowl, beat together the cream cheese and lemon juice. Add onion, salt, liquid smoke, crackers and salmon. (Add another spoonful of cracker crumbs if your mixture seems too sticky). Chill several hours or overnight. Spread out a piece of waxed paper and put a very light coat of flour on it. Make a roll with the salmon mixture. Then roll in the pecans and parsley mixture. Roll onto another piece of waxed paper to be able to lift the roll. Chill several hours and serve with crackers.

This is so good, you'll make it all year long!

Asparagus Rolls

20 thin slices white bread
1 (8 ounce) package cream cheese, softened
3 tablespoons margarine, softened
1 egg
½ teaspoon seasoned salt
20 canned asparagus spears, drained
1½ sticks margarine, melted

Remove crusts from bread and flatten slices with a rolling pin. In mixer bowl combine cream cheese, margarine, egg and seasoned salt. Spread mixture evenly over bread slices. Place an asparagus spear on each one and roll up. Dip in melted margarine to coat all sides. Place on cookie sheet and freeze until ready to bake. Preheat oven to 400 degrees. Cut frozen rolls into thirds and bake for 15 minutes or until lightly browned. Serve immediately.

Sizzling Cheese Squares

1½ cups grated mozzarella cheese
¼ cup real bacon bits
¼ cup mayonnaise
⅓ cup chopped black olives
1 tablespoon chives
⅛ teaspoon cayenne pepper
¼ bell pepper, finely chopped
1 loaf party rye bread

In a medium bowl, combine cheese, bacon bits, mayonnaise, black olives, chives, cayenne pepper and bell pepper. Spread on slices of rye bread. Melt under broiler about 5 minutes. Serve hot.

Green Eyes

4 large dill pickles
4 slices boiled ham
Light cream cheese
Black pepper

Dry off pickle. Lightly coat one side of the slices of ham with the cream cheese and sprinkle a little pepper on each slice. Roll the pickle up in the slice of ham coated with cream cheese and pepper. Chill. Cut into circles to serve.

Cheese Crisps

2 sticks margarine, softened
2 cups grated sharp Cheddar cheese
2 cups flour
2 cups Rice Krispies
½ teaspoon salt
¼ teaspoon garlic powder
¼ teaspoon cayenne pepper

Preheat oven to 350 degrees. Combine margarine and cheese together in mixing bowl; beat well. Add all other ingredients. Mix well and drop by teaspoon onto a ungreased cookie sheet. Bake for 15 minutes or until slightly brown. Cool and store in covered container.

You can do anything. You just can't do everything.—B. J.

Sausage and Pineapple Bits

1 pound link (cooked) sausage
1 pound hot bulk sausage
1 (8 ounce) can crushed pineapple
1 cup apricot preserves
1 cup packed brown sugar
1 tablespoon white wine Worcestershire

Slice link sausage into ¼ inch pieces. Shape bulk sausage into one inch balls. In a skillet, brown sausage balls. In a large saucepan, combine pineapple, preserves, brown sugar and white Worcestershire. Heat and add both sausages. Simmer for 30 minutes. Serve in chafing dish with cocktail picks.

This is fun eating!

Hot Crab Toasts

1 (6 ounce) can white crabmeat, drained
1 (5 ounce) jar Old English cheese spread, softened
¾ stick margarine, softened
1 teaspoon garlic powder
¾ teaspoon seasoned salt
English muffins, halved

Combine crabmeat, cheese spread, margarine, garlic powder and salt. Mix well, using a fork is easiest. Spread over English muffin halves. Place on a baking sheet and bake at 400 degrees for 10 to 15 minutes. Quarter each half to serve. This can be spread and placed in refrigerator; then heated just before serving. If you want to quarter them before heating, check them at 10 minutes. These are great hot or at room temperature.

Crazy Corn Nachos

1 tablespoon oil
⅓ cup finely diced bell pepper
½ cup finely diced onion
⅔ cup fresh whole kernel corn
1 (4 ounce) can chopped green chilies
1 (8 ounce) carton sour cream
1 (8 ounce) package cream cheese, softened
1 teaspoon chili powder
1 teaspoon ground cumin
⅛ teaspoon cayenne pepper (optional)
½ teaspoon salt
2 cups grated Monterey Jack cheese
Tortilla chips
Thinly sliced jalapeno peppers

In a large skillet, heat oil and lightly sauté bell pepper, onion and corn. Stir in green chilies. In a medium mixer bowl, beat together the sour cream, cream cheese, chili powder, cumin, cayenne pepper and salt. Fold mixture into sautéed vegetables. Place chips on baking sheet. Spread vegetable mixture on chips. Sprinkle Monterey jack cheese on top. Place one slice of the jalapeno pepper on top. Broil 2 to 3 minutes or until cheese is melted.

Sort of different. People like the change.

Cocktail Ham Roll-Ups

1 (3 ounce) package cream cheese, softened
1 teaspoon finely grated onion
Mayonnaise
1 (3 ounce) package sliced ham
1 (15 ounce) can asparagus spears

Combine cream cheese, grated onion and enough mayonnaise to make spreading consistency. Separate sliced ham, spread mixture on slices and place an asparagus spear on ham and roll. Cut each roll into 4 pieces. Spear each piece with a toothpick for serving. Refrigerate.

Deviled Egg Spread

3 hard-boiled eggs, mashed
1 (3 ounce) package cream cheese, softened
4 ounces grated Monterey Jack cheese
½ cup mayonnaise
½ teaspoon prepared mustard
¼ teaspoon salt
½ teaspoon white pepper
¾ cup finely grated chopped pecans
1 (4 ounce) can chopped green chilies

In mixing bowl, combine eggs, cream cheese, Monterey Jack cheese, mayonnaise, mustard, salt and pepper; beat well. Add chopped pecans and green chilies; mix. Refrigerate. This makes great sandwiches on dark rye bread

*A fun way to use this spread is to quarter small
green bell peppers and fill with Deviled Egg Spread.*

Caper Cheese Spread

2 (8 ounce) packages cream cheese, softened
1 stick margarine, softened
5 green onions, chopped, tops too
2½ tablespoons finely chopped capers
2½ tablespoons sweet pickle relish
3 tablespoons finely chopped ripe olives
1 teaspoon garlic powder
1 teaspoon paprika
⅛ teaspoon cayenne pepper

Place cream cheese and margarine in mixer bowl and beat until fluffy. Add remaining ingredients, mixing well. Cover and refrigerate for 24 hours or more. Serve with fancy crackers or make small sandwiches with Pumpernickel bread.

Seafood Spread

1 (8 ounce) package cream cheese, softened
⅓ cup mayonnaise
⅓ cup sour cream
3 hard-boiled eggs, mashed
1 (8 ounce) can crabmeat, flaked
1 (8 ounce) can thinly cut shrimp, drained and chopped
¼ onion, very finely chopped
1 rib celery, very finely chopped
1 teaspoon Creole seasoning
Several dashes Tabasco

Combine cream cheese, mayonnaise, sour cream and boiled eggs in mixer bowl. Beat until fairly smooth. Add crabmeat, shrimp, onion, celery, Creole seasoning and Tabasco; mix well.

This can also be used as a dip or to make good sandwiches.

Hot Artichoke Spread

1 (14 ounce) can artichoke hearts, drained and chopped
1 (4 ounce) can chopped green chilies
1 cup mayonnaise
1 cup grated mozzarella cheese
¼ teaspoon white pepper
½ teaspoon garlic salt
Paprika

Remove any spikes or tough leaves from artichoke hearts. Combine all ingredients and mix well. Place in Pam sprayed 9 inch baking dish and sprinkle with paprika over top. Bake at 300 degrees for 30 minutes. Serve warm with tortilla chips or crackers.

Crab and Artichoke Spread

1½ cups freshly grated Parmesan cheese
1 (14 ounce) can artichoke, drained and chopped
1½ cups mayonnaise
½ cup finely minced onion
½ teaspoon Worcestershire
¼ cup fine breadcrumbs
⅛ teaspoon garlic powder
2 drops, Tabasco (optional)
1 (6 ounce) can crabmeat, drained and flakes
Paprika

Mix together the Parmesan cheese, artichoke, mayonnaise, onion, Worcestershire, breadcrumbs, garlic powder, Tabasco and crabmeat. Spread onto a buttered 9 inch glass pie plate. Sprinkle a good amount of paprika over the spread. Bake at 350 degrees for 20 minutes. Serve with crackers.

Cucumber Dip

1 (8 ounce) package cream cheese, softened
1 package Hidden Valley Ranch Dressing mix
1 ½ cucumbers, peeled, grated (scoop out seeds)
¼ cup mayonnaise
1 teaspoon lemon juice
½ cup finely chopped pecans
½ teaspoon salt
¼ teaspoon garlic powder
A scant ⅛ teaspoon cayenne pepper

Combine all ingredients and refrigerate. Serve with chips.

Quick Tuna Dip

1 (7 ounce) can white meat tuna, drained, separated with a fork
1 (1.25 ounce) envelope onion soup mix
1 cup sour cream

⅓ cup finely chopped pecans
⅛ teaspoon cayenne pepper

Combine all ingredients and mix well. Chill several hours before serving. Serve with crackers.

Take time to learn what your mother knows.—BCJ

Spinach-Vegetable Dip

1 (10 ounce) package frozen, chopped spinach, thawed
1 (1 5/8 ounce) package Knorr Swiss vegetable soup mix
½ onion, very finely chopped
1 rib celery, finely chopped
1 cup mayonnaise
1 cup sour cream

Drain spinach very well by pressing out all excess water. (The dip will be too thin if you don't get out the excess water.) Combine all ingredients and mix well. Cover and refrigerate overnight. Serve with crackers or chips.

Dipper's Delight

1 (8 ounce) package cream cheese, softened
2 tablespoons milk
1 (2.5 ounce) package smoked, sliced, pressed
pastrami, cut into very fine pieces
3 green onions, finely sliced, tops too
3 tablespoons finely chopped green pepper
¼ teaspoon black pepper
⅓ cup mayonnaise
½ cup finely chopped pecans
½ teaspoon Tabasco
¼ teaspoon garic powder
¼ teaspoon seasoned salt
½ teaspoon Italian herbs

In mixer bowl, whip together the cream cheese and the milk until creamy. Add remaining ingredients and mix well. Refrigerate. Serve with crackers.

This is so good you'll want to make it into a sandwich!

25

Southwestern Dip

2 (8 ounce) packages cream cheese, softened
¼ cup lime juice
1 tablespoon cumin
1 teaspoon salt
1 teaspoon cayenne pepper
1 (8 ounce) can whole kernel corn, drained
1 cup chopped green chilies
3 green onion, chopped, tops too

In mixing bowl, whip cream cheese until fluffy; beat in lime juice, cumin, salt and cayenne pepper. Stir in corn, walnuts, green chilies and onions. Refrigerate. Serve with tortilla chips.

Try this – you will love it!

Elegant Crab Dip

1 (6 ½ ounce) can white crabmeat, drained
1 (8 ounce) package cream cheese
1 stick butter (the real thing)

In saucepan, combine crabmeat, cream cheese and butter. Heat and mix thoroughly. Transfer to hot chafing dish. Serve with chips.

*This is really delicious and **easy** too!*

Horsey Shrimp Dip

1 (8 ounce) package cream cheese, softened
2/3 cup mayonnaise
1 tablespoon lemon juice
3 tablespoons creamy horseradish
1/4 cup chili sauce
1/2 teaspoon Creole seasoning
1/4 teaspoon garlic powder
2 (8 ounce) cans shrimp, chopped, drained
2 green onions, chopped, tops too

In mixing bowl, combine cream cheese, mayonnaise, lemon juice, horseradish, chili sauce,Creole seasoning and garlic powder; blend well. Chop shrimp and onions. Add shrimp and onions to cream cheese mixture and blend. Refrigerate. Serve with chips.

Wonder Dip

1/3 cup finely chopped green onions
1/2 cup very finely cut broccoli (tiny florets)
1 (8 ounce) can water chestnuts, drained and coarsely chopped
3/4 cup mayonnaise
3/4 cup sour cream
1 (2.7 ounce) jar crystallized ginger, finely chopped
1/2 cup finely chopped pecans
1/2 teaspoon salt
2 tablespoons soy sauce

Mix all ingredients together. Prepare a day ahead and chill. Serve with wheat crackers.

Sassy Onion Dip

1 (8 ounce) package cream cheese, softened
1 (8 ounce) carton sour cream
½ cup chili sauce
1 package dry onion soup mix

In mixer bowl, beat cream cheese until fluffy. Add remaining ingredients and mix well. Cover and chill. Serve with strips of raw zucchini, celery, carrots or turnips.

Five Layer Dip

1 (16 ounce) can refried beans
1 (8 ounce) carton sour cream
1 (1 ounce) package Ranch dressing mix
1 cup diced tomatoes, drained
1 (4 ounce) can chopped green chilies, drained
½ cup shredded Cheddar cheese
½ cup shredded Monterey Jack cheese
1 (2¼ ounce) can black olives, chopped and drained
Chips

Spread beans on a 10 inch serving platter or a 9 inch glass pie plate. In small bowl combine and mix sour cream and dressing mix; then spread mixture over beans. As you spread each layer make it a little smaller around so it becomes tiered. Mix diced tomatoes and green chilies together and spread over the sour cream. Next sprinkle both cheeses over tomatoes and green chilies. Last, sprinkle olives over top. Refrigerate. Serve with chips.

This is really "different" — unique to the palate!

Hot Crab Dip

1 (8 ounce) package cream cheese
1 (8 ounce) can crab meat, pickled and drained
1 clove garlic, finely minced
½ cup mayonnaise
½ teaspoon prepared mustard
1 teaspoon powdered sugar
½ teaspoon salt
2 tablespoons dry white wine

Place all ingredients in the top of a double boiler. Heat, stirring frequently over hot water until cream cheese is melted. Serve warm with tortilla chips.

Party Shrimp Dip

1 (8 ounce) package cream cheese, softened
½ cup mayonnaise
1 can small shrimp, chopped
1 rib celery, finely chopped
2 green onions, finely chopped
¼ teaspoon garlic powder
1 teaspoon lemon juice
¼ teaspoon salt
¼ teaspoon Creole seasoning

Blend cream cheese and mayonnaise. Stir in shrimp, celery, onion, garlic, lemon juice, salt and Creole seasoning. Mix well and chill thoroughly. Serve with chips or sticks of vegetables.

Mexicali Guacamole Dip or Salad

2 green onions
1 tomato
5 to 6 avocados
2½ teaspoons salt
3 tablespoons lemon juice
3 tablespoons mayonnaise
1 teaspoon salad oil
4 dashes Tabasco
¼ cup picante sauce

On a chopping board, chop fine the onion and tomato. Chop and partially mash the avocados and add the salt, lemon juice, mayonnaise, oil, Tabasco and picante sauce. Mix all ingredients together. For a salad, serve on bed of chopped lettuce. For a dip serve with Tostados.

Leave 1 avocado seed in dip to keep avocados from turning dark.

Shrimp Dip

3 cups cooked, deveined shrimp, finely chopped
2 tablespoons horseradish
¼ cup chili sauce
⅔ cup mayonnaise
½ teaspoon salt
½ teaspoon white pepper

Combine all ingredients and refrigerate. (If shrimp have been frozen, be sure to drain well). Serve with cucumber or zucchini slices.

White Chocolate Party Mix

1 (20 ounce) package white chocolate (or Almond Bark)
2 cups Cap'n Crunch cereal
2 cups Cocoa Puffs cereal
2 cups Corn Chex cereal
1 (12 ounce) jar peanuts
1 cup stick (broken up) pretzels
1 (10 ounce) package plain M & M's

EASY

Slowly melt white chocolate or almond bark in top of a double boiler over simmering water. Combine the cereals, peanuts, pretzels and M & M's in a large bowl. When chocolate has melted, slowly pour the white chocolate over the cereal mixture and stir to evenly coat. With a tablespoon, place spoonfuls on wax paper, cool; or you can spread mixture on wax paper and when it is cool you break into small pieces. Store in airtight container and refrigerate to keep fresh.

I like to put it out in "dabs"- they seem to stay together better.
This is great to put in Christmas tins to give away as a
"thank you" or just "With Love"!

Spiced Pecans

2 cups sugar
½ cup water
2 teaspoons cinnamon
¼ teaspoon salt
1 teaspoon ground nutmeg
½ teaspoon ground cloves
4 cups pecan halves

Combine all ingredients except pecans in deep dish. Mix well and cover with waxed paper. Microwave on high for 4 minutes. Stir. Microwave another 4 minutes. Add pecans; quickly mixing well. Spread out on waxed paper to cool. Break apart and store in covered container.

These will disappear! My friend made these for everybody in the bridge club — now we expect 'em every Christmas.

Scotch Crunchies

½ cup crunchy peanut butter
1 (6 ounce) package butterscotch bits
2½ cups Frosted Flakes
½ cup peanuts

Combine peanut butter and butterscotch bits in a large saucepan and melt over low heat. Stir until butterscotch bits are melted. Stir in cereal and peanuts. Drop by teaspoonfuls onto wax paper. Refrigerate until firm. Store in air-tight container.

Pecan Oat Munchies

1 (16 ounce) package Quaker Oat Squares cereal
2 cups whole pecans
½ cup corn syrup
½ cup packed brown sugar
½ stick margarine
1 teaspoon vanilla
½ teaspoon baking soda

Heat oven to 250 degrees. Combine cereal and pecans in a 9 x 13 inch baking pan. Set aside. Combine corn syrup, brown sugar and margarine in a 2 cup bowl. Microwave on high 1½ minutes, stir and turn bowl. Microwave on high about I minute or until boiling. Stir in vanilla and soda. Pour over cereal mixture, stirring well to coat evenly. Bake in oven one hour, stirring every 20 minutes. Spread on baking sheet to cool.

This is great munching!

Crazy Cocoa Crisps

24 ounces white almond bark
2¼ cups Cocoa Krispies
2 cups dry roasted peanuts

Place almond bark in double boiler; heat, while stirring, until almond bark is melted. Stir in cereal and peanuts. Drop by teaspoon on cookie sheet. Store in airtight container.

I've stopped trying to cook like mother. I can follow her recipes, but I can't stir in the memories.
— Erma Bombeck

Texas Party Mix

1 (12 ounce) box corn Chex
1 (12 ounce) box Wheat Chex
1 (12 ounce) box Crispix
1 package thin pretzels
2 cans mixed nuts
2 cans peanuts
2½ sticks margarine
2 tablespoons Lawry's seasoned salt
2 tablespoons garlic powder
2 tablespoons Tabasco
2 tablespoons Worcestershire
2 teaspoons cayenne pepper

Mix first 6 ingredients together in a large roasting pan. Melt margarine and add next 5 ingredients and pour over cereal mixture and stir. Bake at 250 degrees for about 2 hours. Store in air-tight containers.

We lived on this at the lake during the summers.

Haystacks

1 (12 ounce) package butterscotch morsels
2 cups chow mein noodles
1 cup dry roasted peanuts

In a medium saucepan, heat butterscotch morsels over low heat until completely melted. Add noodles and peanuts and stir until each piece is coated. Drop from spoon onto wax paper. Cool.

Amaretto

3 cups sugar
2¼ cups water
1 pint vodka
3 tablespoons almond extract
1 tablespoon vanilla (not the imitation)

Combine sugar and water in a large pan. Bring mixture to a boil. Reduce heat. Let simmer 5 minutes, stirring occasionally. Remove from stove. Add vodka, almond and vanilla. Stir to mix well. Store in airtight jars.

Kahula

3 cups hot water
1 cup instant coffee granules
4 cups sugar
1 quart vodka
1 vanilla bean, split

In a large saucepan combine hot water and coffee; mixing well. Add sugar and bring to a boil. Boil 2 minutes. Turn off heat and cool. Add vodka and vanilla bean. Pour into a bottle or jar and let set for 30 days before serving. Shake occasionally.

If you happen to have some of the Mexican vanilla, you can make "instant" Kahlua by using 3 tablespoons of Mexican vanilla instead of the vanilla bean; then you do not have to wait 30 days.

Nice clothes will take you lots of places. — BCJ

Sparkling Cranberry Punch

Ice mold for punch bowl
Red food coloring, optional
2 quarts cranberry juice cocktail
1 (6 ounce) can frozen lemonade, thawed
1 quart ginger ale, chilled

Pour water in a mold for the ice ring; add red food coloring to make the mold brighter and prettier. Mix cranberry juice and lemonade in pitcher. Refrigerate until ready to serve. When serving, pour cranberry mixture into punch bowl and add the ginger ale, stirring well. Add decorative ice mold to the punch bowl. Serves 24 cups.

Green Party Punch

1 (3 ounce) package lime gelatin
1 cup boiling water
1 (6 ounce) can frozen limeade
1 (6 ounce) can frozen lemonade
1 quart orange juice
1 quart pineapple juice
1 tablespoon almond extract
2 to 3 drops green food coloring
1 liter ginger ale, chilled

Dissolve lime gelatin and boiling water; stirring well. In a gallon bottle, combine dissolved gelatin, limeade, lemonade, orange juice, pineapple juice, almond extract and food coloring. Chill. When ready to serve, add the ginger ale. Serves 32.

This punch would also be a good one to use when the party is close to St. Patrick's Day!

Reception Punch

4 cups sugar
6 cups water
5 ripe bananas, mashed
Juice of 2 lemons
1 (46 ounce) can pineapple juice
1 (6 ounce) can frozen undiluted orange juice
2 quarts ginger ale

Boil sugar and water for 3 minutes. Cool. Blend bananas with lemon juice. Add pineapple and orange juice. Combine all. The ingredients except the ginger ale. Freeze in a large container. To serve thaw 1 ½ hours; then add ginger ale. Punch will be slushy. Serves 40.

Very Special Coffee Punch

1 (2 ounce) jar instant coffee
2 quarts hot water
2¼ cups sugar
2 quarts half and half
1 quart ginger ale
1 pint heavy cream, whipped
½ gallon French vanilla ice cream

Dissolve instant coffee in hot water. Cool; add sugar and half and half, mixing well. Chill. When ready to serve, pour coffee-sugar mixture in punch bowl, add chilled ginger ale, whipped cream and ice cream. Let some chunks of ice cream remain. This will make 60 four ounce servings.

I Promise - This Will Make a Hit!
Everyone will be back for seconds!

Ruby Punch

2 (6 ounce) cans frozen orange juice concentrate
4 cups water
2 (46 ounce) cans red Hawaiian punch
1 (46 ounce) can pineapple juice
1 (48 ounce) bottle cranapple juice
2 liters ginger ale, chilled

In two gallon bottles, combine orange juice, water, Hawaiian punch, pineapple juice and cranapple juice; stir well. Chill. Place in punch bowl. Just before serving, add ginger ale. Makes 2 gallons.

The cranapple juice in this punch really makes it a "Christmas" special!

Party Punch

3 cups sugar
2½ quarts water
1 (6 ounce) package lemon gelatin
1 (3 ounce) can frozen orange juice concentrate, thawed
⅓ cup lemon juice
1 (46 ounce) can pineapple juice
3 tablespoons almond extract
2 quarts ginger ale, chilled

Combine sugar and 1 quart water. Heat until sugar is dissolved. Add gelatin, stirring until dissolved. Add fruit juices, remaining 1½ quarts water and almond extract. Refrigerate. When ready to serve, place in punch bowl and add chilled ginger ale. This will make 50 servings.

The almond extract really gives this punch a special taste!

Rise and shine.

Garlic Herb Bread

1 loaf French bread
1 stick margarine, melted
1 teaspoon dried parsley flakes
½ teaspoon dried crushed oregano
¼ teaspoon dried dill weed
¼ teaspoon garlic powder
Freshly grated Parmesan cheese

Slice bread in thick slices. Mix together the margarine, parsley, oregano, dill weed and garlic. Spread, with a brush, each slice generously with margarine mixture. Sprinkle about ½ teaspoon of the Parmesan cheese on each slice. Reassemble into loaf shape and spread remainder of margarine mixture over the top. Place on a cookie sheet and wrap foil halfway up loaf, leaving top exposed. Bake in a 375 degree oven for about 20 minutes. While cooking, the aroma is heavenly!

French Bread Monterey

1 loaf French bread, sliced
Margarine, softened
1 cup mayonnaise
½ cup grated Parmesan cheese
½ onion, very finely chopped
½ teaspoon Worcestershire
Paprika

Preheat oven to 200 degrees. Spread bread slices completely with margarine and place on a cookie sheet. Mix together mayonnaise, cheese, onion and Worcestershire. Spread mixture on buttered bread, then sprinkle with paprika. Place in oven for 15 minutes, then turn on broiler and delicately brown. Serve immediately.

Texas Garlic Toast

1 loaf French bread
1 tablespoon garlic powder
¼ cup finely chopped parsley or
1 tablespoon dried parsley flakes
1 teaspoon marjoram leaves
1 stick margarine, melted
1 cup Parmesan cheese

Slice bread into 1 inch slices diagonally. In a small bowl combine rest of ingredients except cheese and mix well. Using a brush, spread mixture on bread slices and sprinkle with Parmesan cheese. Place on cookie sheet and bake at 225 degrees for about 1 hour.

Brunch Muffins

1 stick margarine, melted
2 cups self-rising flour
1 (8 ounce) carton sour cream

EASY

Combine all ingredients; mix well. Spoon into miniature muffin tins. Bake at 350 degrees about 25 minutes or until lightly browned. Do not use the large muffin tins.

These make nice little "tea" biscuits for a luncheon.

Butterfingers

2 cups buttermilk baking mix
1 tablespoon dried onion flakes
1 egg
⅓ to ½ cup milk
1 stick butler or margarine
2 tablespoons dried parsley flakes
1 ½ teaspoon Italian seasoning
½ teaspoon paprika
⅓ cup grated Parmesan cheese (optional)

Combine mix, egg and just enough milk to make a thick dough. Turn dough out on a lightly floured surface and knead lightly. Pat into about a 9 x 13 inch rectangle. Heat oven to 375 degrees and place the butter in a 10 x 14 inch pan and melt in hot oven. Cut the dough into about 12 or 14 strips with a sharp knife or pizza cutter. Cut each strip in half. Place strips evenly atop the melted butter (or margarine) in the pan. Combine the parsley flakes. Italian seasoning, paprika and Parmesan cheese; then sprinkle over the strips. Bake for about 10 to 12 minutes, until golden brown. Serve hot. You can make them ahead of time if you need to, then reheat.

These are like breadsticks without going to the trouble of using yeast. Good with pasta or salads too!

We can't help getting old, but we don't have to act like it.
— BCJ

Angel Biscuits

5 cups flour
¼ cup sugar
3 teaspoons baking powder
1 teaspoon soda
1 teaspoon salt
⅔ cup shortening
1 ½ packages dry yeast
¼ cup warm water
2 cups buttermilk
Oil

Sift dry ingredients together. Cut in shortening. Dissolve yeast in warm water and add with buttermilk to dry ingredients. Mix well but only until dough is well moistened. Place in covered bowl and refrigerate to use as needed. To bake biscuits, remove amount desired, roll out on floured board to about ½ inch thickness and cut with biscuit cutter. Place on oiled baking pan, turning once to grease both sides. Bake at 400 degrees until nicely browned, about 12 to 15 minutes. Remaining dough will keep in refrigerator for 2 weeks.

Mexican Spoon Bread

1 cup yellow cornmeal
1 tablespoon sugar
1 teaspoon salt
½ teaspoon baking soda
⅓ cup oil
2 eggs, beaten
1 (16 ounce) can cream style corn
1 (4 ounce) can chopped green chilies
¾ cup milk
2 cups grated Cheddar cheese

Preheat oven to 350 degrees. In mixing bowl, combine and mix cornmeal, sugar, salt and baking soda. Stir in milk and oil; mix well. Add eggs and corn; mix well. Spoon one half of the batter into a greased 9 x 13 inch baking pan. Sprinkle one half the green chilies and one half the cheese over batter. Repeat layers, ending with cheese. Bake uncovered for 45 minutes or until lightly browned. To serve, this should be spooned from the pan. It would serve as a substitute for potatoes or rice.

Crunchy Bread Sticks

1 package hot dog buns
2 sticks margarine, melted
Garlic powder
Paprika
Parmesan cheese

Take each half bun and slice in half lengthwise. Using a pastry brush, butter all bread sticks and sprinkle a light amount of garlic powder and just a few sprinkles of paprika and Parmesan cheese. Place on cookie sheet and bake at 225 degrees for about 45 minutes. It is good to have these made up and frozen. When you can take out just the number you want and warm them up.

You won't believe how good these are and easy too!

Sesame Toast

2 tablespoons sesame seeds
2 tablespoons margarine
1 stick margarine
¼ teaspoon basil
½ teaspoon rosemary
¼ teaspoon marjoram
½ teaspoon garlic powder
½ loaf French bread

In a medium saucepan, brown sesame seeds in 2 tablespoons margarine. Add stick of margarine; melt and add seasonings. Let stand overnight in refrigerator. When ready to make toast, stir the margarine mixture and spread mixture on bread slices. Bake at 300 degrees for 20 minutes or until slightly browned.

Squash Cornbread

1 cup yellow cornmeal
1 cup flour
2 tablespoons light brown sugar
5 teaspoons baking powder
1 teaspoon salt
½ teaspoon ground cumin
1 tablespoon dried parsley flakes
3 dashes cayenne pepper
1 grated zucchini or yellow squash (about 1 cup)
2 eggs
1 cup milk
¼ cup oil
¾ cup grated Cheddar cheese
1 (4 ounce) can chopped green chilies

In a large bowl, mix together cornmeal, flour, brown sugar, baking powder, salt, cumin, parsley and cayenne pepper. Add the squash, eggs, milk, oil, cheese and green chilies. Mix well. Pour into a greased 9 x 13 inch baking pan. Cook at 400 degrees for 25 to 30 minutes or until lightly browned. Serves 8 to 10.

When the strongest words for what I have to offer come out of me sounding like words I remember from my mother's mouth, then I either have to reassess the meaning of everything I have to say now, or re-examine the worth of her old words.
— Audre Lorde

Just Plain Ole Cornbread

1 cup flour
1 cup yellow cornmeal
¼ cup sugar
4 teaspoons baking powder
¾ teaspoon salt
2 eggs
1 cup milk
¼ cup oil

Mix all ingredients together; blend well. Pour into a greased 9 x 13 inch baking pan. Bake at 375 degrees for 30 minutes or until lightly browned.

Wonderful Strawberry Bread

3 cups flour
2 cups sugar
1 teaspoon salt
1 teaspoon baking soda
2 teaspoons cinnamon
3 large eggs, beaten
1 cup oil
1¼ cups chopped pecans
2 (10 ounce) packages frozen sweetened strawberries, undrained

Combine dry ingredients into a large mixing bowl. Add eggs and oil, mix thoroughly. Fold in pecans and strawberries. Mix well. Pour into 2 greased and floured 5 x 9 inch loaf Pans. Bake in a preheated 325 degree oven for one hour and 10 minutes. Test with toothpick to make sure bread is done. Let cool several minutes before removing from pan.

Wonderful toasted for breakfast or with the Pineapple Pecan Spread.

Pineapple Pecan Spread

2 (8 ounce) packages cream cheese, softened
1 (8 ounce) can crushed pineapple, drained, but save juice
¾ cup chopped pecans

In mixer bowl, beat cream cheese. Add the drained pineapple, stir by hand and add just enough of the juice to make the mixture spreadable. Add pecans. Refrigerate. This is good on most any of the dessert breads.

48

Banana Pineapple Loaf

2 sticks margarine, softened
2 cups sugar
4 eggs
1 cup mashed ripe bananas
3¾ cups flour
2 teaspoons baking powder
2 teaspoon baking soda
½ teaspoon salt
1 (15 ounce) can crushed pineapple, undrained
½ cup coconut, optional
1 cup chopped pecans

Cream margarine and sugar. Add eggs and beat until fluffy. Stir in bananas. Combine all dry ingredients and add to margarine mixture (it will be stiff). Fold in pineapple, coconut and pecans. Pour into 2 greased and floured 5 x 9 inch loaf pans. Bake in a preheated 325 degree oven for 1 hour and 10 to 15 minutes. Test with toothpick to make sure bread is done. Let cool several minutes before removing from pan.

Wonderful toasted for breakfast or with the Spicy Orange Butter.

Spicy Orange Butter
2 sticks butter, softened
1 cup powdered sugar
2 teaspoons orange juice
½ teaspoon ginger
¼ teaspoon nutmeg
½ teaspoon cinnamon
½ cup orange peel
1½ teaspoon orange extract

Mix all ingredients together and store in refrigerator. Let stand several minutes at room temperature before serving.

Coconut Bread

1 ¼ cups shredded coconut
2⅔ cups flour
1 ¼ cups sugar
4 teaspoons baking powder
1 teaspoon salt
1 egg
2 tablespoons oil
1 ¼ teaspoons coconut extract

Place coconut on an ungreased cookie sheet and bake for 15 minutes at 300 degrees. Shake the pan and stir 2 times so that it will be evenly toasted. Remove from oven and cool. Turn oven temperature up to 350 degrees and coat a 9 x 5 inch loaf pan with Pam.

Sift flour, sugar, baking powder and salt into a mixing bowl. Stir in coconut. In a 2 cup measuring cup (or just a small container) combine milk, egg, oil and coconut extract. Beat a little to get the egg mixed into the milk. Add the liquid mixture all at once and stir until well blended. Do not over mix. Pour batter into the prepared loaf pan and bake at 350 degrees for 1 hour and 5 minutes. Check with toothpick to make sure it is done in the middle. Cool. To serve, cut in thin slices and spread with Strawberry Butter. Place another slice on top. Cut in 3 strips.

It makes a pretty plate of red and white sandwiches.

Strawberry Butter

1 ¼ cups powdered sugar
1 (10 ounce) package frozen strawberries, defrosted
1 cup butter, softened

Place all ingredients in a food processor and process until well blended. Chill and spread on bread. It would be good served on biscuits and muffins too.

This is also very good on your morning toast. Tastes more like fresh strawberries than strawberry preserves.

Island Mango Bread

2 cups flour
1 teaspoon baking soda
1 teaspoon cinnamon
¼ teaspoon salt
1 cup sugar
3 eggs, beaten
¾ cup oil plus 1 tablespoon
2 cups peeled, seeded and finely diced mangoes (takes 2 ripe mangoes)
1 teaspoon lemon juice
⅓ cup coconut
⅔ cup chopped pecans

Grease and flour two 8 x 4 inch loaf pans (that is a small loaf pan). In a large bowl, combine flour, soda, cinnamon, salt and sugar. Mix. In a separate bowl, stir together the eggs, oil, mangoes and lemon juice. Pour into flour mixture and mix well, by hand. Stir in coconut and pecans. Pour into prepared pans. Bake at 350 degrees for 40 to 45 minutes. Test at 40 minutes to see if it is done.

This is a wonderful, moist and delicious bread —
great toasted for breakfast!

Sweet Apple Loaf

⅔ cup margarine
2 cups sugar
4 eggs
2 cups canned applesauce
⅓ cup milk
1 tablespoon lemon juice
4 cups flour
1 teaspoon cinnamon
2 teaspoons baking powder
1 teaspoon baking soda
1 teaspoon salt
1½ cups chopped pecans
¾ cup chopped maraschino cherries, well drained

Cream together margarine, sugar and eggs and beat several minutes. Stir in applesauce, milk and lemon juice. Sift together flour, cinnamon, baking powder, baking soda and salt; add to first mixture and mix well. Fold in pecans and cherries. Pour into 3 greased and floured loaf pans. Bake at 325 degrees for 1 hour. Test with toothpick for doneness. Let stand 10 to 15 minutes, then remove from pans and cool on rack. Freezes well. Serve toasted for breakfast or spread with cream cheese for lunch.

Mincemeat Bread

1¾ cups flour
1¼ cups sugar
2½ teaspoons baking powder
½ teaspoon salt
2 eggs, beaten
1 teaspoon vanilla
1 ½ cups prepared mincemeat
¾ cups pecans
⅓ cup shortening, melted

Glaze:
1 cup powdered sugar
1 tablespoon milk
¼ cup finely chopped pecans

In a large bowl combine flour, sugar, baking powder and salt. In medium bowl combine eggs, vanilla, mincemeat and pecans. Mix well. Stir in the melted shortening; mixing quickly. Batter will be stiff. Pour egg mixture into dry ingredients. Stir only enough to moisten flour. Spoon batter into a greased and floured loaf pan. Bake at 350 degrees for 1 hour or until toothpick inserted in center comes out clean. Cool 15 minutes and remove from pan. Cool completely. Mix powdered sugar and milk and stir until smooth. Stir in pecans. Spread over the top of loaf. Slice bread and spread a little margarine on each slice and toast.

This bread is well worth the cost of the prepared mincemeat. It usually comes in a large jar so you will have enough left to make the mincemeat cookies. They are delicious.

Applesauce Pecan Bread

1 cup sugar
1 cup applesauce
⅓ cup oil
2 eggs
2 tablespoons milk
1 teaspoon almond extract
2 cups flour
1 teaspoon soda
½ teaspoon baking powder
¾ teaspoon cinnamon
¼ teaspoon salt
¼ teaspoon ground nutmeg
¾ cup chopped pecans

Topping:
½ cup chopped pecans
½ teaspoon cinnamon
½ cup packed brown sugar

Combine sugar, applesauce, oil, eggs, milk and almond extract. Mix well. Combine all dry ingredients and add to sugar mixture; mix well. Fold in pecans. Pour into greased and floured loaf pan. For topping, combine pecans, cinnamon and brown sugar. Sprinkle over batter. Bake at 350 degrees for 1 hour and 5 minutes. Test for doneness. Cool on rack.

When you talk too much, you're the only one interested in what you're saying. — BCJ

Apricot Bread Extraordinaire

3 cups flour
1½ teaspoons baking soda
½ teaspoon salt
2 cups sugar
1 ½ cups oil
4 eggs
1 (5 ounce) can evaporated milk
1¼ cups apricot butter
1¼ cups chopped pecans

Apricot Butter:
1¼ cups finely chopped apricots, soaked overnight in water
1 cup sugar

Mix together flour, baking soda and salt. Add sugar, oil, eggs, and vanilla. Mix together flour and evaporated milk. Mix thoroughly. Add apricot butter and pecans; blend. Pour into 2 greased and floured loaf pans and bake at 350 degrees for 1 hour and 5 to 10 minutes or until loaf tests done.

To make Apricot Butter, soak apricots overnight in water to cover. Add sugar and simmer 10 minutes or until soft. Cool completely before adding to recipe.

This is "it " for apricot lovers!

Apple Banana Bread

3 apples, peeled, grated
3 bananas, mashed
2 teaspoons lemon juice
1 stick margarine, softened
2 cups sugar
2 eggs
3 cups flour
1½ teaspoons baking powder
1½ teaspoons baking soda
⅓ teaspoon salt
1 teaspoon vanilla

Sprinkle apples and bananas with lemon juice. In a mixing bowl, cream together margarine, sugar and eggs and beat well. Stir in fruit. Add dry ingredients and vanilla. Stir. Pour into 2 greased and floured loaf pans. Bake at 350 degrees for 50 to 55 minutes or until golden brown.

Ginger Muffins

1½ stick margarine, softened
¾ cup sugar
¼ cup corn syrup
¼ cup sorghum molasses
2 eggs
1 teaspoon baking soda
½ cup buttermilk
2 cups flour
Pinch of salt
1 teaspoon ground ginger
¼ teaspoon cinnamon
¼ cup raisins, optional
½ cup chopped pecans

In a mixing bowl, combine margarine, sugar, syrup and molasses; beat well. Add eggs; beat well. Stir soda into buttermilk; add to mixture and beat. Add flour, salt, ginger and cinnamon. Beat. Stir in raisins and pecans; mix well. Pour into 20 to 24 greased muffin tins and bake at 350 degrees for 16 to 18 minutes or more according to the size of muffins.

The mother is the one supreme asset of national life. She is more important, by far, than the successful statesman or businessman or artist or scientist.
—Theodore Roosevelt

Apricot Pineapple Muffins

⅓ cup very finely cut up dried apricots
1 stick margarine, softened
1 cup sugar
1 egg
1 (8 ounce) can crushed pineapple, undrained
1¼ cups flour
½ teaspoon baking soda
½ teaspoon salt
½ cup quick rolled oats

Cut apricots up with your kitchen scissors. Set aside. With mixer, cream margarine and sugar together. Add egg and pineapple; beat well Add all dry ingredients; mixing well. Fold in apricots. Spoon into well greased muffin tins (or use the paper liners) and bake at 350 degrees for 20 minutes. Makes 12 muffins.

This is a winner!

Hidden Secret Muffins

Filling:
1 (8 ounce) package cream cheese, softened
1 egg
⅓ cup sugar
1 tablespoon grated orange rind

Muffin:
2 sticks margarine, softened
1 ¾ cups sugar
3 eggs
3 cups flour
2 teaspoons baking powder
1 cup milk
1 teaspoon almond extract
1 cup chopped, toasted almonds

Beat cream cheese, eggs, sugar and orange rind together; set aside. Cream margarine and sugar until light and fluffy. Add eggs one at a time, beating after each addition. Stir flour and baking powder together. Add flour and milk alternately to margarine and sugar mixture, beginning and ending with flour. Add almond extract and fold in almonds. Fill 26 lightly greased muffin tins half full of muffin batter. Spoon about 1 heaping tablespoon of filling in each muffin tin. Top filling with muffin batter. Bake muffins at 375 degrees for 20 to 25 minutes or until muffin just bounces back when pressed and until they are lightly browned.

These are what my Daddy would have called "Larripin good"!

Maple Spice Muffins

1¼ cups flour
1½ cups whole wheat flour
½ cup quick-cooking oats
1 teaspoon baking soda
2 teaspoons baking powder
2 teaspoons cinnamon
½ teaspoon ground cloves
2 eggs
1 (8 ounce) carton sour cream
1 cup maple syrup
1 cup packed brown sugar
½ cup oil
½ teaspoon maple flavoring (optional)
1 banana, mashed
1 cup chopped walnuts

Preheat oven to 375 degrees. In a mixing bowl, combine the flours, oats, soda, baking powder, cinnamon and cloves; mix. Add eggs, sour cream, maple syrup, brown sugar, oil, maple flavoring and mashed banana. Stir well by hand. Add walnuts and pour into 24 paper lined muffin tins. Bake for 18 to 20 minutes.

If you don't try, you'll never know
whether or not you can do it. — BCJ

Yummy Muffins

1½ margarine, softened
¾ sugar
¼ corn syrup
¼ cup sorghum molasses
2 eggs
1 teaspoon baking soda
½ cup buttermilk
2 cups flour
Pinch of salt
1 teaspoon ground ginger
¼ teaspoon cinnamon
¼ cup raisins, optional
½ cup chopped pecans

In a mixing bowl, combine margarine, sugar, syrup and molasses; beat well. Add eggs; beat well. Stir soda into buttermilk; add to mixture and beat. Add flour, salt, ginger and cinnamon. Beat. Stir in raisins and pecans; mix well. Pour into 20 to 24 greased muffin tins and bake at 350 degrees for 16 to 18 minutes or more according to the size of muffins.

Applesauce Spice Muffins

2 sticks margarine, softened
1 cup packed brown sugar
1 cup granulated sugar
2 eggs
1¾ cups applesauce
2 teaspoons cinnamon
1 teaspoon allspice
½ teaspoon ground cloves
½ teaspoon salt
2 teaspoons baking soda
3½ cups flour
1½ cups chopped pecans

Cream together the margarine and sugars. Add eggs, applesauce, spices, salt, baking soda and flour. Mix well. Add pecans; stir will. Pour into 28 greased muffin tins or pans with paper liners. Bake at 375 degrees for 16 minutes.

Light and Crispy Waffles

EASY

2 cups biscuit mix
1 egg
½ cup oil
1⅓ cups club soda

Start waffle iron heating. Combine all ingredients in a medium mixing bowl and stir by hand. Pour just enough batter to cover waffle iron. This batter can also be used for pancakes. To have waffles for a "company weekend," make up all waffles. Freeze separately on cookie sheet; place in large baggies. To heat, place in a 350 degree oven for about 10 minutes.

Graham Streusel Coffee Cake

2 cups graham cracker crumbs
¾ cup chopped pecans
¾ cup firmly packed brown sugar
1½ teaspoons cinnamon
¾ cup margarine, melted
1 (18-ounce) package yellow cake mix
1 cup water
¼ cup oil
3 eggs

Glaze:
1½ cups powdered sugar
2 tablespoons water

Mix crumbs, pecans, brown sugar, cinnamon and margarine; set aside. Blend cake mix, water, oil and eggs on medium speed for about 3 minutes. Pour half of batter into a greased and floured 9 x 13 inch pan; sprinkle with half of the reserved crumb mixture. Spread remaining batter evenly over crumb mixture; sprinkle with remaining crumb mixture. Bake at 350 degrees for 45 to 50 minutes. Cool. Mix powdered sugar and water and drizzle glaze over cake.

Cherry-Nut Breakfast Cake

1 (8 ounce) package cream cheese
2 sticks margarine, softened
1½ cups sugar
1½ teaspoons vanilla
3 eggs
2¼ cups flour
1½ teaspoons baking powder
1 (10 ounce) jar maraschino cherries, drained
½ cup chopped pecans

Glaze:

1½ cups powdered sugar
2½ tablespoons milk
2 tablespoons margarine, melted
½ teaspoon almond extract
½ cup chopped pecans

In a large mixing bowl, blend cream cheese, margarine, sugar, vanilla and eggs. Beat 3 minutes. Add flour and baking powder and beat well. Cut each cherry into 3 or 4 pieces; then fold in cherries and ½ cup chopped pecans. Pour batter into a greased and floured 9 x 13 inch baking pan and bake at 350 degrees for 40 minutes. Just before cake is done, mix together the powdered sugar, milk, melted margarine and almond extract. Glaze while cake is still warm. Top with remaining ½ cup pecans.

French Apple Coffee Cake

¾ cup sugar
1 cup packed light brown sugar
⅔ cup buttermilk
2 eggs
2½ cups flour
2 teaspoons soda
2 teaspoons cinnamon
½ teaspoon salt
1 can apple pie filling
¼ cup white raisins
1 stick margarine, melted

Topping:
1 teaspoon cinnamon
¼ cup sugar
⅓ cup packed light brown sugar
⅔ cup chopped walnuts

Mix by hand the sugars, buttermilk and eggs. Add the flour, baking soda, cinnamon and salt, mixing well. (I like the apple slices to be in smaller pieces so I empty the can of Pie filling in a plate and cut each slice in half. Fold in pie filling and raisins. Pour into a greased and floured 9 x 13 inch baking pan and spread out. Combine all the topping ingredients and sprinkle over top of cake. Bake in a 350 degree preheated oven for 45 minutes. Will serve 12 big squares.

When cake is done, drizzle the melted margarine over top of the cake. Serves 12

This is an excellent cake to have on hand for Sunday morning or when you have out-of-town company. It is rich and moist and just needs a cup of steaming hot coffee to go with it.

Cranberry Crown Coffee Cake

½ cup margarine, softened
1 cup plus 2 tablespoons sugar
2 eggs
2 cups, flour
1 teaspoon baking powder
1 teaspoon baking soda
1 (8 ounce) carton sour cream
1 teaspoon almond extract
1 (16 ounce) can whole cranberry sauce
¾ cup chopped slivered almonds

Glaze:

¾ cup powdered sugar
1 to 2 teaspoons water
1 teaspoon almond extract

Grease and flour a bundt or tube pan. Cream together the margarine and sugar with electric mixer. Beat in eggs one at a time. Mix together the dry ingredients. Add dry ingredients alternately with the sour cream. Stir in almond extract. Spoon one half of the batter into the prepared pan. In a small bowl stir the cranberry sauce so that it is spreadable. Spread three-fourths of the cranberry sauce over the batter and sprinkle one half of the almonds. Pour the remaining batter on top; then spoon the remaining cranberry sauce and almonds on top. With a long knife, cut through and swirl batter and cranberries. Bake in a 350 degree oven for 60 minutes. Cool for about 20 minutes before removing cake from pan. When cake is cool, mix all glaze ingredients together; mixing until smooth. Drizzle on cake.

Good Morning Coffee Cake

2⅓ cups flour
1½ cups sugar
¾ teaspoon salt
¾ cup shortening
2 teaspoons baking powder
¾ cup milk
2 eggs
1 teaspoon vanilla
1 (3 ounce) package cream cheese, softened
1 can sweetened condensed milk
⅓ cup lemon juice
1 can peach pie filling
2 teaspoons cinnamon
¾ cup chopped pecans

In a mixing bowl, combine flour, sugar and salt; cut in shortening until crumbly. Reserve I cup crumb mixture. To remaining crumb mixture, add baking powder, milk, eggs and vanilla. Beat on medium speed for 2 minutes. Spread into a greased and floured 9 x 13 inch baking dish. Bake at 350 degrees for 25 minutes. In another bowl, beat cream cheese and condensed milk until fluffy; gradually fold in lemon-juice, peach pie filling and cinnamon. Spoon this mixture over cake that has cooked 25 minutes. With the remaining crumb mixture, add pecans and sprinkle on top of cake. Bake 30 minutes longer. Serve warm.

Apricot Coffee Cake

2 sticks margarine, softened
1 (3 ounce) package cream cheese
1½ cups sugar
2 eggs
1 teaspoon vanilla
1½ teaspoons baking powder
2¼ cups flour
1 can apricot pie filling*

Icing:
1½ cups powdered sugar
2 tablespoons milk
2 tablespoons margarine, melted
½ teaspoon almond extract

In a mixing bowl combine the margarine, cream cheese and sugar; beat together at low speed. Add eggs and vanilla and beat together at medium speed. Add baking powder and flour and beat well. Spread 1/3 of the batter in a greased and floured 9 x 13 inch baking pan. Spread pie filling over batter. Using a teaspoon, drop remaining batter over pie filling. Bake at 350 degrees for 40 to 45 minutes. Cool. Mix powdered sugar, milk, margarine and almond extract together and beat until smooth. Drizzle icing over cake. *Other pie fillings may be used.

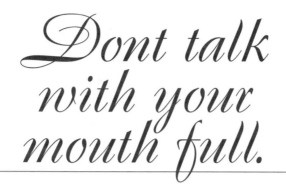

Dont talk with your mouth full.

The Ultimate Cheddar Cheese Soup

1 cup finely chopped onion
1 red bell pepper, diced
2 tablespoons margarine
1 pound extra sharp Cheddar cheese, grated
2 tablespoons cornstarch
1 can chicken broth
1½ cups ham, diced
1½ cups broccoli flowerets, cooked
¾ cup diced and cooked carrots
1 teaspoon Worcestershire sauce
¼ teaspoon salt
¼ teaspoon white pepper
½ teaspoon garlic powder
2 cups half and half

In a large saucepan, sauté the onion and bell pepper in the margarine. Mix together the cheese and the cornstarch. To the onion and peppers, add the broth, then the cheese-cornstarch mixture a little at a time; heat and cook until cheese has melted. Stir until smooth. Add the ham, broccoli, carrots, Worcestershire, salt, white pepper and garlic powder. Heat over low heat while adding the half and half. Serve with a sprig of watercress. Serves 6 to 8.

Chicken Tortellini Soup

6 large chicken breasts, boned and cooked
3 (10½ ounce) cans chicken broth
1 cup chopped celery
1 large onion, chopped
2 cans cream of chicken soup
I (16 ounce) package frozen chopped broccoli
1 (9 ounce) package fresh cheese tortellini
½ teaspoon black pepper
1 teaspoons basil
½ teaspoon Italian seasoning
¼ teaspoon garlic powder
1 (8 ounce) carton sour cream

Save the chicken broth that the chicken was cooked in; you might want to thin the soup. In a large stockpot, combine canned chicken broth, celery and chopped onion, cook until tender, about 15 minutes. Add the chicken soup, broccoli, cheese tortellini, pepper, basil, Italian seasoning and garlic powder. Bring to boiling point, turn heat down and simmer 15 minutes. Stir in the sour cream. This makes a fairly thick soup so if you want it thinner, add a cup of the chicken broth that the chicken was cooked in.

This is "Comfort Food" at its best!

A mother starts out as the most
important person in her child's life and
eventually becomes the stupidest.
— Mary Kay Blakely

Cream of Zucchini Soup

1 small onion, finely chopped
2 tablespoons margarine
3½ cups unpeeled, grated zucchini
1 (14½ ounce) can chicken broth
1 teaspoon seasoned salt
1 teaspoon dill weed
½ teaspoon white pepper
1 (8 ounce) carton sour cream

In a saucepan, sauté onion in margarine until onion is just lightly cooked, but not brown. Add zucchini, broth, seasoned salt, dill weed and pepper to the onion. Bring to boiling point, turn heat down and simmer 15 minutes. Stir in sour cream; mix well and bring to boiling point, but do not boil. Remove from heat and serve. Serves 4 to 8.

Asparagus Soup

½ stick margarine
3 cans chicken broth
¾ teaspoon garlic powder
1 bunch green onions, diced (some tops too)
1 large potato, cut up into small chunks
½ (8 ounce) package Velveeta cheese, cut in chunks
1 (15 ounce) can extra long asparagus spears
1 (8 ounce) carton sour cream

Combine margarine, broth, garlic, green onion and potato in large saucepan. Heat and cook until potatoes are tender, approximately 15 minutes. Add Velveeta cheese and leave on heat just long enough for the cheese to melt. Cut the asparagus

(Continued on Next Page)

(Continued)

spears into one inch lengths and add to soup. Fold in so
cream and heat (do not boil) just enough to make the soup ho
This may be made the day before. If you want a spicy soup, use
mild Mexican Velveeta instead of the plain Velveeta. Serves 6 to
8. For garnish, you can sprinkle Bacos on top of soup when
serving.

Incredible Broccoli Cheese Soup

1 (10 ounce) box frozen chopped broccoli
3 tablespoons margarine
¼ onion, finely chopped
¼ cup flour
1 (16 ounce) carton half and half
1 (14 ounce) can chicken broth
½ teaspoon salt
¼ teaspoon black pepper
⅛ teaspoon cayenne pepper
½ teaspoon summer savory
½ (1 pound) box mild Mexican Velveeta cheese, cubed

Punch several holes in the box of broccoli and microwave for 5
minutes. Turn box in microwave and cook another 4 minutes.
Leave in Microwave for 3 minutes. In a large saucepan, melt
margarine and sauté the onion; do not brown. Add flour, stir;
then gradually add half and half, chicken broth and seasonings.
Stirring constantly; heat until mixture has thickened slightly.
Do not let this come to a boil. Add chunks of cheese and heat
while stirring, until cheese is melted. Add cooked broccoli.
Serve piping hot. Serves 4 to 6.

This really is an incredible soup! For a "soup" dinner, I
sometimes use it with the Pancho Villa Stew on page 77 and
make small sandwiches using the the Seafood Spread on page 22.
It's fun watching people decide which is best. Most can't stop
eating the soup.

Corn and Ham Chowder

3 medium potatoes
2 cans chicken broth, divided
5 tablespoons margarine
2 ribs celery, chopped
1 onion, chopped
4 tablespoons flour
1 (4.5 ounce) can chopped green chilies
½ teaspoon white pepper
½ teaspoon salt
1 teaspoon seasoned salt
¼ teaspoon garlic powder
1 (16 ounce) package frozen corn
1 (16 ounce) can cream style corn
1 pint half and half
3 cups bite-sized cubed ham
2 cups shredded Cheddar cheese

Peel potatoes and cut in small chunks. Cook with one of the cans of chicken broth. In a large kettle, melt margarine an sauté the celery and onion. Add the flour, stir. Pour in the other can of chicken broth and heat, stirring constantly until slightly thickened. Add the drained, cooked potatoes and the remaining ingredients. Heat slowly, stirring several times to keep from sticking. This will only serve 6 to 8 because everyone will want a second bowl.

This is a great recipe to use when you have left-over ham!

Zesty Chicken Cream Soup

¼ stick margarine
½ onion, finely chopped
1 carrot, grated
1 (10 ounce) can cream of celery soup
1 (10 ounce) can cream of mushroom soup
1 (10 ounce) can cream of chicken soup
1 (14 ounce) can chicken broth
2 soup cans milk
1 tablespoon parsley flakes
¼ teaspoon garlic powder
1 (1 pound) box mild Mexican Velveeta cheese, cubed
4 chicken breasts, cooked and diced*

In a large saucepan or roaster, melt margarine and sauté onion and carrots for about 10 minutes; do not brown. Add all remaining ingredients. Heat, but do not boil; turn heat to medium-low and cook, stirring constantly, until cheese is melted. Serve piping hot. *Leftover turkey could be substituted for chicken. Serves 8.

This is really the "easy" way to make chicken soup and if you are in an absolute rush, you could use 2 of the large cans of chicken.

Cadillac Chili

Oil
1½ pounds lean ground beef
2 pounds chili ground beef
1 onion, chopped
1 (15 ounce) can tomato sauce
1 (10 ounce) can diced tomatoes and green chilies
4 tablespoons ground cumin
1 teaspoon oregano
2 tablespoons chili powder
1 tablespoon salt
2 cups water
1 (15 ounce) can pinto beans, undrained, optional

In a little oil, combine meats and onion in a large kettle or roaster. Brown. Add all remaining ingredients except beans. Bring to a boil; reduce heat and simmer for 2 hours. Add beans; heat. Serve with crackers or cornbread. Beans could be heated separately. Place about 2 tablespoons on top of bowl of chili when served.

Pancho Villa Stew

3 cups diced, cooked ham
1 pound smoked sausage, cut in ½ inch slices
3 cans chicken broth
1 (15 ounce) can whole tomatoes, undrained
3 (4 ounce) cans chopped green chilies, undrained
1 large onion, chopped
1 teaspoon garlic powder
2 teaspoons ground cumin
2 teaspoons cocoa
1 teaspoon dried oregano
½ teaspoon salt
2 (15 ounce) cans pinto beans, undrained
1 (15 ounce) can hominy, undrained
1 (8 ounce) can whole kernel corn, undrained
Flour tortillas

In a roaster, combine ham, sausage, chicken broth, tomatoes, green chilies, onion, garlic powder, cumin, cocoa, oregano and salt. Bring to a boil, reduce heat and simmer 45 minutes. Add pinto beans, hominy and corn, bring to a boil; reduce heat and simmer another 15 minutes. Serve with buttered flour tortillas (or cornbread, that's good too).

Spicy Turkey Soup

3 to 4 cups chopped turkey
3 (10 ounce) cans condensed chicken broth, undiluted
2 (10 ounce) cans diced tomatoes and green chiles
1 (16 ounce) can whole corn
1 large onion, chopped
1 (10 ounce) can tomato soup
1 teaspoon garlic powder
1 teaspoon dried oregano
3 tablespoons cornstarch
3 tablespoons water

In a large roaster, combine turkey, broth, tomatoes and green chilies, corn, onion, tomato soup, garlic powder and oregano. Mix cornstarch with the water and add to soup mixture. Bring to boiling, then reduce heat and simmer, stirring occasionally about 2 hours. Yield about 2½ quarts.

This is spicy – but not too much, just right! Try it with chicken, too.

Ham Chowder

1 cup sliced celery
½ cup chopped onion
2 tablespoons margarine
3 cups shredded cabbage
3½ cups fully cooked diced ham
2 (16 ounce) cans Mexican style stewed tomatoes, undrained
1 (15 ounce) can whole kernel corn, drained
1 (15 ounce) can whole potatoes, drained and sliced
1 can condensed chicken broth, undiluted
1 cup water
½ cup ketchup
¼ cup packed light brown sugar
½ teaspoon salt
½ teaspoon garlic powder

In a large roaster or soup kettle, over medium heat, sauté celery and onion in the margarine. Add remaining ingredients; bring to a boil. Reduce heat; cover and simmer for 1 hour

This is a real "tasty" way to use left-over ham - a good flavor!

If you can't beat them, charm them. — BCJ

Taco Soup

1½ pounds lean ground beef
1 onion, chopped
1 package taco seasoning
1 (16 ounce) can whole kernel corn, undrained
1 (16 ounce) can pinto beans, undrained
1 (16 ounce) can stewed tomatoes, undrained
1 cup water
1 (14 ounce) can beef broth
Chopped chives for garnish
Sour cream for garnish

In a large roaster, combine beef and chopped onion; brown, stirring well. Add Taco seasoning, corn, beans, tomatoes, water and broth; stir well. Bring to boiling point, then turn heat down and simmer for 2 hours. Or, it could be cooked in a crock pot all day. Ladle soup into bowls; garnish with chives and a dollop of sour cream. Serve with tortilla chips. Serves 8.

Santa Fe Stew

1½ pounds ground round
1 package taco seasoning
1 package Original Ranch Dressing mix
1 (15 ounce) can whole kernel corn
1 (15 ounce) can kidney beans
2 (15 ounce) cans stewed tomatoes
2 (15 ounce) cans pinto beans
1 can Rotel chilies and tomatoes

Brown the ground meat and drain is necessary. Add both packages of seasoning and mix well. Add (undrained) the corn,

(Continued on Next Page)

(Continued)

kidney beans, stewed tomatoes, pinto beans and Rotel; Mix well and simmer about 25 minutes. If you want it really hot, use 2 cans of the Rotel and tomatoes. Serve with cornbread or the broccoli cornbread.

Tortilla Soup

1 onion, chopped
1 (14 ounce) can chopped green chilies
2 cloves garlic, minced
2 tablespoons oil
1 cup tomatoes, peeled and chopped
1 bell pepper, chopped
1 (14 ounce) can beef broth
1 (14 ounce) can clear chicken broth
1½ cups water
1½ cups tomato juice
1 teaspoon cumin
2 teaspoons chili powder
1 teaspoon coriander
1 teaspoon salt
1 teaspoon freshly ground pepper
2 teaspoons Worcestershire
6 corn tortillas, cut into ½ inch strips
1 cup grated Cheddar cheese

Sauté onion, chilies and garlic in oil until soft. Add tomatoes, bell pepper, beef and chicken broth, water, tomato juice, cumin, chili powder, coriander, salt, pepper and Worcestershire. Bring soup to a boil; lower heat and simmer, covered for 1 hour. Just before ready to serve, add tortillas and cheese and simmer for 10 minutes. Serves 6.

Potato Cheese Soup

4 large potatoes, cubed
2 carrots, sliced
Water
2 stalks celery, sliced
1 onion, finely grated
½ stick margarine
3 tablespoons instant chicken bouillon
1 teaspoon seasoned salt
¼ teaspoon ground thyme
½ teaspoon crushed rosemary
¼ teaspoon garlic powder
½ teaspoon white pepper
2 cups half and half
1½ cups grated Cheddar cheese
3 slices bacon, cooked and chopped

In a large saucepan cook potatoes and carrots with just enough water to cover vegetables. When cooked mash with a potato masher or a mixer (do not drain water off). Carrots will remain chunky. In a small saucepan, sauté celery and onions in margarine. Add to mashed potatoes in the large saucepan. Add remaining ingredients except bacon. Bring to a boil, lower heat and simmer for 10 minutes. Serve with bacon pieces sprinkled over individual bowls of soup. Serves 6 to 8.

Black Bean Soup

2 cups dried black beans, washed, soaked overnight and drained
1 cup diced ham
1 onion, chopped
1 carrot, chopped
2 stalks celery, chopped
3 jalapeno peppers, seeded and chopped
2 (14½ ounce) cans chicken broth
10 cups water
2 teaspoons cumin
1 teaspoon salt
2 tablespoons snipped fresh cilantro
1 teaspoon oregano
1 teaspoon chili powder
I teaspoon cayenne pepper
1 (8 ounce) carton sour cream

In a large, heavy soup pot, place all ingredients except sour cream. Bring to a boil; turn heat down and simmer for about 3 hours or until beans are tender. Add more water as needed and stir occasionally; make sure there is enough water in pot to make soup consistency and not too thick. Place a few cups at a time in a food processor (using the steel blade) or the blender and puree it until it is smooth. Add sour cream and reheat soup. Serve in individual bowls.

A man's work is from sun to sun, but a
mother's work is never done.

— Anonymous

White Lightning Chili

1½ cups dried navy beans
3 (14 ounce) cans chicken broth
¼ stick margarine
1 cup water
1 onion, chopped
1 clove garlic, minced
3 cups chopped, cooked chicken
1 (4 ounce) can chopped green chilies
½ teaspoon sweet basil
½ teaspoon white pepper
1½ teaspoons ground cumin
½ teaspoon dried oregano
⅛ teaspoon cayenne pepper
⅛ teaspoon ground cloves
6 (8 inch) flour tortillas
Grated Monterey Jack cheese
Salsa, optional

Sort and wash beans; place in a Dutch oven. Cover with water 2 inches above beans. Soak overnight. Drain beans. Add broth, margarine, water, onion and garlic. Bring to a boil; reduce heat and cover. Simmer 2½ hours, stirring occasionally. With potato masher, mash beans several times so that about half of the beans are mashed. Add chicken, green chilies, basil, white pepper, cumin, oregano, cayenne pepper and cloves. Bring to a boil; reduce heat and cover. Simmer another 30 minutes. With kitchen shears, make 4 cuts in each tortilla toward center, but not through center. Line serving bowls with tortillas, overlapping cut edges. Spoon in chili and top with cheese or salsa.

Cucumber Sandwiches

1 (8 ounce) package cream cheese, softened
1 tablespoon mayonnaise
1 teaspoon lemon juice
1 package Hidden Valley Ranch Dressing mix (dry)
½ teaspoon salt
⅛ teaspoon cayenne pepper
½ teaspoon garlic powder
1 tablespoon dry parsley flakes
2 cucumbers, peeled and grated (scoop out seeds)
White sandwich bread

In mixer bowl, beat cream cheese, mayonnaise and lemon juice until it is creamy. Add the dressing mix, salt, cayenne pepper, garlic powder and parsley flakes; mix well. Prepare cucumbers and combine all ingredients. Cut crusts off bread and spread sandwiches. Keep refrigerated.

Grilled Bacon and Bananas

Peanut butter
8 slices English muffins
2 bananas
8 slices bacon, crispy cooked
Margarine, softened

Spread a layer of peanut butter over 8 slices of muffins. Slice bananas and arrange on top of 4 slices. Place 2 strips bacon on each of the 4 slices. Top with remaining muffin slices. Spread top slice with margarine. Brown sandwiches, margarine side down. Spread top slices with margarine. Turn and cook the other side until golden brown. Serve hot.

Spinach Sandwiches

0 ounce) packages frozen chopped spinach, thawed
1 (8 ounce) package cream cheese, softened
1 cup mayonnaise
2 boiled eggs, mashed
1 box Knox vegetable soup mix (dry)
¾ cup chopped pecans

Drain spinach VERY well - then mash it to squeeze out more water - then press it between several pieces of paper towels. Place cream cheese in mixer bowl and beat until smooth; add mayonnaise and beat until they are well mixed. Stir in the mashed eggs, Knox vegetable soup mix and pecans. Let stand in refrigerator several hours before spreading sandwiches. This makes enough to make up a large loaf of bread into sandwiches.

Hot Bunwiches

8 hamburger buns
8 slices Swiss cheese
8 slices ham
8 slices turkey
8 slices American cheese

Now you can have Sunday night supper ready in the freezer. Lay out all 8 buns. On the bottom, place the slices of Swiss cheese, next the ham, next the turkey and last, the American cheese. Place the top bun over the American cheese. Wrap each Bunwich individually in foil and place in freezer. When ready to serve, take out of freezer 2 to 3 hours before serving. Heat in a 325 degree oven for about 30 to 40 minutes. Serve hot. Variations: Instead of ham and turkey, try using some of the good thin-sliced deli meats such as pastrami, corned beef, etc. Switch the cheese to slices of Mexican cheese.

Swiss Tuna Grill

1 (7 ounce) can white tuna, drained, flaked
½ cup shredded Swiss cheese
1 rib celery, finely chopped
¼ onion, finely chopped
¼ cup mayonnaise
¼ cup sour cream
½ teaspoon seasoned salt
¼ teaspoon pepper
Rye bread
Margarine, softened

Combine tuna, Swiss cheese, celery, onion, mayonnaise, sour cream, seasoned salt and pepper; mix well. Spread on rye bread; top with another slice of rye bread. Spread top of sandwiches with margarine and place on a hot griddle. On medium heat, brown tops and bottoms of sandwiches. Serve hot.

Party Cheese Fingers

12 slices whole wheat bread
2½ cups grated sharp Cheddar cheese
⅓ cup chili sauce
¾ cup mayonnaise
½ cup chopped olives
½ cup chopped pecans
1 (2 ounce) jar chopped pimentos
¼ teaspoon garlic powder

Trim crusts off bread. Combine all remaining ingredients and mix well. Spread mixture on 6 slices of bread. Top with remaining bread slices. Cut each sandwich into 3 strips. Refrigerate.

Reuben Sandwiches

½ cup mayonnaise
1 tablespoon chili sauce
12 slices rye bread
12 slices corned beef
6 slices Swiss cheese
1 (16 ounce) can sauerkraut, well drained
Margarine, softened

Mix mayonnaise and chili sauce; spread over 6 slices of the rye bread. Then a slice of corned beef, cheese, a second slice of corned beef and the sauerkraut. Top with remaining bread slices. Spread top slices of bread with a layer of margarine. Place sandwiches, margarine side down, in skillet. Spread top of bread with margarine. Cook uncovered over low heat until bottom is golden brown - about 10 minutes. Turn; cook until golden brown and cheese is melted.

Green Chili Puff

10 eggs
½ cup flour
1 teaspoon baking powder
½ teaspoon salt
1 (16 ounce) carton small curd cottage cheese
½ pound mozzarella cheese
1 bunch green onion, chopped (tops too)
½ pound Cheddar cheese
1 stick margarine, melted
1 (7 ounce) can chopped green chilies

Preheat oven to 350 degrees. Beat eggs until light and lemon colored. Add flour, baking powder and salt and beat until smooth. Add cottage cheese, mozzarella cheese, green onions Cheddar cheese, melted margarine and green chilies. Stir until well mixed. Pour into a Pam sprayed 9 x 13 inch baking pan. Bake for about 40 minutes or until top is slightly brown around edges and center appears firm. Serve immediately. Salsa can be served on the side. Serves 12.

This recipe is so versatile! You can cut it in little squares and serve warm as an appetizer or serve it for a brunch or for lunch. It would go well with a Mexican meal - morning, noon or night!

God couldn't be everywhere, and
therefore he made mothers.
— Jewish Proverb

ـ؟ple-Cheese Casserole

ıce) cans pineapple chunks, drained
1 cup sugar
5 tablespoons flour
1½ cups grated Cheddar cheese
1 stack Ritz Crackers
1 stick margarine, melted

Grease a 9 x 13 inch baking dish and layer in the following order: 1. Pineapple 2. Sugar-flour mixture, 3. Grated cheese, 4. Cracker crumbs, 5. Margarine drizzled over casserole. Bake at 350 degrees for 25 minutes or until bubbly.

This would be good served at a brunch or luncheon or as a side dish to sandwiches or ham. And also great served at a morning bridge club along with a coffee cake or the delicious strawberry bread.

Cinnamon Soufflé

1 loaf cinnamon raisin bread
1 (20 ounce) can crushed pineapple, undrained
2 sticks margarine, melted
½ cup sugar
5 eggs, slightly beaten
½ cup chopped pecans

Slice a very thin amount of the crusts off. Then tear the bread into small pieces and place in a buttered 9 x 13 inch pyrex dish. Pour pineapple and juice over the bread and set aside. Cream together the margarine and sugar. Add eggs to creamed mixture and mix well. Pour the creamed mixture over the bread and pineapple. Bake, uncovered, for 40 minutes. Serve hot or warm. Serves 10 to 12.

Breakfast Bake

1 pound hot sausage, cooked and crumbed
2 tablespoons dried onion flakes
1 cup grated Cheddar cheese
1 cup Bisquick
¼ teaspoon salt
¼ teaspoon pepper
4 eggs
2 cups milk

Preheat oven to 350 degrees. Place cooked and crumbled sausage in a Pam sprayed 9 x 13 inch glass baking dish. Sprinkle with onion flakes and cheese. In mixing bowl, combine Bisquick, salt, pepper and eggs. Beat well. Add milk and stir until fairly smooth. Pour over sausage mixture. Bake for 35 minutes. If you want to make one day and cook the next morning, just keep refrigerated before cooking. To cook the next morning, add an extra 5 minutes to the cooking time since you would be taking it right out of the refrigerator. Serves 8. For a bunch, add 1 (8 ounce) can of whole corn, drained.

This is my family's all-time favorite Christmas morning breakfast. Of course you have to have biscuits too! Just make your biscuits with "biscuit baking mix" and milk. Cook them but do not brown them. Cool and stick them in the freezer so you won't have to work on Christmas morninig. Just brown them in the oven.

Quick Quiche

1 stick margarine, melted
1½ cups half and half
½ teaspoon salt
¼ teaspoon pepper
3 green onions, chopped, tops too, optional
½ cup biscuit mix
1 cup grated Swiss cheese
¾ cup chopped ham
4 eggs, beaten

Preheat oven to 350 degrees. Grease a 10 inch pie plate. Combine melted margarine, milk, salt, pepper, green onions and biscuit mix. Blend well with mixer. Pour into a 10 inch pie plate. Sprinkle batter with cheese and ham. Push meat below the surface with the back of a spoon. Beat eggs in the same mixer bowl and pour over the ham and cheese. Bake for 40 minutes. Let sit at room temperature about 10 minutes before slicing. Serves 6 to 8.

Quesadilla Pie

1 (4 ounce) can chopped green chilies
½ pound sausage, cooked
2 cups grated Cheddar cheese
3 eggs, well beaten
1½ cups milk
¾ cup biscuit mix
Hot salsa

Spray a 9 inch pie pan with Pam. Sprinkle the green chilies in pie pan; then cooked sausage and Cheddar cheese. In a separate bowl, mix together the eggs, milk and biscuit mix. Pour over the chilies, sausage and cheese. Bake in preheated 350 degree oven for 30 minutes. Serve with salsa on top of each slice. Serves 6.

Sausage and Chilies Quiche

1 (9 inch) uncooked pie shell
1 (7 ounce) can whole green chilies
1 pound hot sausage, cooked, crumbled, drained
4 eggs, slightly beaten
2 cups half and half
½ cup grated Parmesan cheese
¾ cup grated Swiss cheese
½ teaspoon salt
¼ teaspoon pepper

Preheat oven to 350 degrees. Line bottom of pie shell with split and seeded green chilies. Sprinkle sausage over chilies. Combine eggs, cream, cheeses, salt and pepper. Pour over sausage. Cover edge of pastry with foil to prevent excessive browning. Bake for 35 minutes or until top is golden brown. Allow quiche to set out of oven 5 minutes before serving.

Ham and Cheese Bars

2 cups Bisquick
1 heaping cup cooked, finely chopped ham
4 ounces Cheddar cheese, grated
½ onion, finely chopped
½ cup grated Parmesan cheese
¼ cup sour cream
½ teaspoon salt
1 teaspoon garlic powder
1 cup milk
1 egg

Preheat oven to 350 degrees. Grease a 9 x 13 inch baking pan. Combine all ingredients in a mixing bowl and mix by hand. Spread in baking pan and bake 30 minutes or until lightly brown. Cut in rectangles, about 2 inches by 1 inch. These are good made for a brunch or lunch, using as a bread. These are good to keep in refrigerator (cooked) and re-heated to serve. Heat at 325 degrees for about 20 minutes; they will be good and crispy heated a second time.

Dont be sassy.

Merry Mix Salad

EASY

3 (15 ounce) cans fruit cocktail, undrained
1 (14 ounce) can pineapple chunks
2 (3.4 ounce) packages coconut cream instant pudding mix
(dry)
1 cup pecan halves, slightly broken up by hand
1 can cherry pie filling
1 (8 ounce) carton Cool Whip
A few drops of red food coloring

In a very large bowl, mix the fruit cocktail, pineapple chunks and coconut pudding mix together. Add the pecans and cherry pie filling, then fold in the Cool Whip with the drops of red food coloring. Place in a pretty crystal bowl and cover. For company, you could use this as a dessert - just spoon this into parfait glasses, cover with Saran Wrap and have it ready in the refrigerator.

I don't know why we call this a salad, because it is so good —
it's Dessert! The friend, who gave me this recipe, keeps a
recipe made up in the freezer to have ready when needed to
take to a friend. Kids love it too! Sooo easy!

Mama exhorted her children at every opportunity
to "jump at de sun". We might not land on the sun,
but at least we would get off the ground.

— Zora Neale Hurston

Strawberry Cream

1 can strawberry pie filling
1 can Eagle Brand condensed milk
1 (8 ounce) carton Cool Whip
1 (15 ounce) can crushed pineapple, undrained
1 cup chopped pecans
1 cup tiny marshmallows
¼ teaspoon almond extract
1 tablespoon lemon juice

Combine all ingredients in a large mixing bowl and gently mix.
Refrigerate. It can also be used as a dessert. Serves 12.

Orange Fluff Salad

1 (12 ounce) carton small curd cottage cheese
1 (3 ounce) package orange gelatin
1 (11 ounce) can mandarin oranges, drained
1 (15 ounce) can crushed pineapple, drained
½ cup coconut
½ cup chopped pecans
1 (8 ounce) carton Cool Whip

In a large mixing bowl, combine cottage cheese and dry orange
gelatin and mix well. Stir in oranges, pineapple, coconut and
pecans. Fold in Cool Whip. Refrigerate. Serve in a pretty crystal
bowl.

Fantastic Fruit Salad

2 cans mandarin oranges
2 (15 ounce) cans pineapple chunks
1 (16 ounce) package frozen strawberries, thawed and drained
1 can peach pie filling
1 can apricot pie filling
2 bananas, sliced

Drain oranges, pineapple and strawberries. In a mixing bowl, combine oranges, pineapple, strawberries, peach pie filling, apricot pie filling and bananas; gently mix together. Place in a beautiful crystal bowl for serving. This is a wonderful fruit salad for special holiday dinners. Serves 16.

My niece always takes this to her office Christmas dinner. Her co-workers keep requesting this fruit salad — year after year!

Creamy Fruit Salad

1 can sweetened condensed milk
¼ cup lemon juice
1 can peach pie filling*
1 (15 ounce) can pineapple chunks, drained
2 (15 ounce) cans fruit cocktail, drained
1 cup chopped pecans
1 (8 ounce) carton Cool Whip

In a large bowl, combine condensed milk and lemon juice. Stir until well mixed. Add the pie filling, pineapple chunks, fruit cocktail and pecans. Mix. Fold in Cool Whip. Serve in a can substitute any other pie filling. Serves 12 to 14.

This will get you requests for more — it's so easy, you can oblige!

Frozen Holiday Salad

2 (3-ounce) packages cream cheese, softened
2 tablespoons mayonnaise
2 tablespoons sugar
1 (16-ounce) can whole cranberry sauce
1 (8-ounce) can crushed pineapple, drained
½ cup chopped pecans
1 cup tiny marshmallows
1 (8-ounce) carton Cool Whip

In mixer bowl combine cream cheese, mayonnaise and sugar; beat until creamy. Add fruit, pecans and marshmallows. Fold in Cool Whip and pour into a greased 9 x 13 inch shallow Pyrex dish and freeze. When ready to serve, take salad out of freezer a few minutes before cutting into squares.

Snowball Salad

1½ cups sugar
1 (8 ounce) carton sour cream
2 tablespoons lemon juice
1 (8 ounce) carton Cool Whip
1 (15 ounce) can crushed pineapple, drained
2/3 cup maraschino cherries, cut in several pieces
1 cup chopped pecans
3 bananas, mashed

Mix together the sugar, sour cream and lemon juice. Fold in remaining ingredients and pour into a 9 x 13 inch glass dish. Freeze. When ready to serve, take out of freezer about 10 or 15 minutes before trying to slice.

My testers loved this dish and said they could eat it as a dessert as well as a salad!

Lime Mint Salad

2 (16 ounce) cans crushed pineapple, drained
1 (6 ounce) package lime flavored gelatin
1 (10 ounce) package tiny marshmallows
1 (12 ounce) carton Cool Whip
1 teaspoon pineapple extract
½ teaspoon mint extract
1 (8 ounce) box buttermints, crushed

Mix pineapple, dry gelatin and marshmallows in bowl and let set overnight at room temperature. Next day fold in Cool Whip, pineapple extract, mint extract and buttermints. Pour into a 9 x 13 pyrex dish and freeze. Set out of freezer a few minutes before cutting and serving. Serves 12.

The buttermints make this recipe a special treat.

Incredible Strawberry Salad

2 (8 ounce) packages cream cheese, softened
2 tablespoons mayonnaise
½ cup powdered sugar
1 (16 ounce) package frozen strawberries, thawed
1 (10 ounce) package small marshmallows
1 (8 ounce) can crushed pineapple, drained
1 (8 ounce) carton Cool Whip
1 cup chopped pecans

In a large mixing bowl, combine cream cheese, mayonnaise and powdered sugar. Beat until creamy. Fold in strawberries (if strawberries are large, cut them in half), marshmallows, pineapple, Cool Whip and pecans. Pour into a 9 x 13 inch glass dish. Freeze. Take out of freezer about 15 minutes before cutting and serving. Serves 12.

It really is incredible!

Champagne Salad

¾ cup powdered sugar
1 (8 ounce) package cream cheese, softened
1⅓ cups maraschino cherries, cut in half, well drained
1 (20 ounce) can crushed pineapple, drained
2 bananas, mashed
1 (8 ounce) carton Cool Whip
1 cup chopped pecans
1½ cups miniature marshmallows

Cream together sugar and cream cheese. Fold in cherries, pineapple, bananas, Cool Whip, pecans and marshmallows; mix well. Pour into a Pam sprayed 9 x 13 inch pan and freeze. Thaw 15 minutes before trying to cut in squares to serve.

This is a great "make ahead" salad!

Dreamy Apricot Salad

2 (3 ounce) packages apricot gelatin
1 cup boiling water
1 (8 ounce) package cream cheese, softened
1 (14 ounce) can sweetened condensed milk
2 (15 ounce) cans apricot halves, drained
1 (20 ounce) can crushed pineapple, undrained
1½ cups chopped pecans

Dissolve gelatin in boiling water, stirring until gelatin is well dissolved. Cool. Beat cream cheese with beater until fairly smooth, then add condensed milk and beat until smooth. Cut each apricot half into about 6 to 8 pieces. To the cooled gelatin mixture, add cream cheese mixture, apricots, pineapple and pecans. Pour into a Pam sprayed 9 x 13 inch dish. Refrigerate. Serves 12.

Divinity Salad

1 (6 ounce) package lemon gelatin
¾ cup boiling water
1 (8 ounce) package cream cheese
2 tablespoon sugar
¾ cup chopped pecans
1 (15 ounce) can crushed pineapple, undrained
1 (8 ounce) carton Cool Whip

In mixer bowl, mix gelatin with boiling water until gelatin is dissolved. Cool slightly. Add cream cheese; beat at very slow speed at first! Add sugar, pecans and pineapple. Cool. Fold in Cool Whip. Pour into a 9 x 13 inch pan. Refrigerate. Serves 12.

This is my favorite salad. I love to serve it with the Shrimp and English Pea Salad on page 144 and the Pine Nut Green Beans on page 150.

Apricot Cream Salad

1 (6-ounce) package apricot or orange flavored gelatin
2 (17-ounce) cans apricots, reserve liquid
1 (6-ounce) can mandarin oranges, drained
2 cups tiny marshmallows

Topping:
1 (8-ounce) package cream cheese, softened
1½ cups milk
1 (4 ounce) package instant vanilla pudding
½ cup grated cheese

Dissolve gelatin in 1½ cups of boiling apricot juice (if not enough juice, add water or orange juice to make 1½ cups). Add fruits and marshmallows and pour into a greased 9 x 13 inch

(Continued on Next Page)

(Continued)

glass dish and let congeal. For topping; whip cream cheese and add milk and pudding and beat until smooth. Spread mixture over congealed salad. Top with grated cheese and cover with plastic wrap. Chill and cut into squares to serve. Serves 10 to 12.

Christmas Salad

1 (6 ounce) package lime gelatin
1 (8 ounce) can crushed pineapple, drained juice
from pineapple plus water to make 1 cup
1 (8 ounce) package cream cheese, softened
1 cup miniature marshmallows
1 (8 ounce) carton Cool Whip
1 (6 ounce) package raspberry gelatin
1 cup boiling water
1 (12 ounce) package frozen raspberries, thawed
1 (8 ounce) can crushed pineapple, undrained

Dissolve lime gelatin in a large mixing bowl with 1 cup of boiling pineapple juice and water. Add cream cheese and beat on slow speed of mixer. Fold in marshmallows and pineapple. Cool in refrigerator about 30 minutes and fold in Cool Whip. Pour into Pam sprayed 9 x 13 inch glass dish and refrigerate until set. In separate bowl, dissolve raspberry gelatin with the boiling water. Add raspberries and crushed pineapple; pour over first layer of gelatin mixture. Refrigerate until firm. If you like strawberries better than raspberries, use strawberries and of course change the raspberry gelatin to strawberry gelatin.

Pink Poinsettia Salad

1 (6 ounce) package raspberry gelatin
1 cup boiling water
1 can blueberry pie filling
1 (8 ounce) can crushed pineapple, undrained
1 cup chopped pecans
1 (8 ounce) carton Cool Whip

Dissolve gelatin in boiling water, stirring well. Stir in pie filling, crushed pineapple and pecans. Set in refrigerator for about 30 minutes to cool. When chilled, fold in Cool Whip. Pour into a Pam sprayed 9 x 13 inch glass dish. When ready to serve, cut in squares and serve on a lettuce leaf. Serves 12.

This makes a very pretty salad for a luncheon. Pretty plus delicious!

Mincemeat Salad

1¾ cups orange juice
1 (6 ounce) package lemon gelatin
2 cups prepared mincemeat
1 cup chopped celery
1 cup chopped pecans
1 (15 ounce) can crushed pineapple, drained
1 medium apple, diced
1 tablespoon lemon juice

Heat orange juice. Add gelatin; stir until dissolved. Stir in mincemeat, celery, pecans and pineapple. Sprinkle lemon juice over apple and toss. Add to other ingredients. Pour into a Pam sprayed 9 x 13 inch glass dish. Chill. Serves 12.

Berry Pizzaz

1 (6 ounce) package blackberry gelatin
1 cup boiling water
1 (8 ounce) can crushed pineapple, undrained
1 can blueberry pie filling

Topping:
1 (8 ounce) package cream cheese, softened
1 (6 ounce) carton blueberry yogurt
Chopped pecans

In a mixing bowl, dissolve gelatin in boiling water; stirring well. Fold in pineapple and pie filling. Pour into a 9 x 13 inch dish. Chill until firm. For topping, beat together the cream cheese and yogurt; spread on top of gelatin mixture. Top with chopped pecans. Serves 8.

Cherry Cranberry Salad

1 (6 ounce) package cherry gelatin
1 cup boiling water
1 can cherry pie filling
1 (16 ounce) can whole cranberry sauce

In mixing bowl, combine cherry gelatin and boiling water; mix until gelatin is dissolved. Mix pie filling and cranberry sauce into gelatin. Pour into a 9 x 13 inch baking dish and refrigerate. Serve on lettuce leaves. Serves 8 to 10.

What could be easier? – Nothing! Don't wait to serve this only at Christmas and Thanksgiving – use it anytime of the year.

Cinnamon Salad

3 cups water
2 (6 ounce) packages cherry gelatin
1/3 cup cinnamon red hot candies
1 (25 ounce) jar applesauce
2 teaspoons lemon juice

Filling:
2 (8 ounce) packages cream cheese, softened
1 cup mayonnaise
1 cup chopped walnuts

In a large saucepan, heat water to boiling; add gelatin and stir until dissolved. Lower heat to moderately low and add candies. Continue heating and stirring until candies are dissolved. Remove from heat; add applesauce and lemon juice. Pour half gelatin mixture into a 9 x 13 inch baking dish. Set aside remaining gelatin mixture at room temperature. Place first layer in freezer for about an hour or until set. In a mixer bowl, combine cream cheese and mayonnaise until fairly smooth. Mix in walnuts. When first layer of gelatin is set, spread cream cheese mixture over top. Chill about 30 minutes; then pour remaining gelatin mixture over cream cheese layer. Refrigerate several hours. Serve on lettuce leaves. Serves 15.

Pistachio Salad

1 (15-½ ounce) can crushed pineapple, drained
1 (11-ounce) can mandarin oranges, drained
1 (6-ounce) package pistachio pudding
2 cups miniature marshmallows
1 cup chopped pecans
1 cup coconut, optional
1 (12-ounce) carton Cool Whip

Mix first 6 ingredients and then fold in Cool Whip. Refrigerate. Serve in a crystal bowl. Serves 8 to 10.

Perfect to serve on St. Patrick's Day.

Mango Salad

1 (3 ounce) package apricot gelatin
2 (3 ounce) package lemon gelatin
1¾ cups boiling water
1 (8 ounce) package cream cheese, softened
2 (15 ounce) cans mangoes, with juice

In a medium size bowl, dissolve both gelatin in the boiling water. In mixer bowl, beat the cream cheese well, until very creamy. Add the mangoes and juice and beat (the canned mangoes are soft and will beat well) until the mangoes are just like pieces. Add mango mixture into the gelatin and pour into a 2 quart mold that has been sprayed with Pam. It will make 12 to 14 little individual molds if you prefer.

This could make a delightful light dessert molded in a sherbet dish with a little shortbread cookie placed on the dessert plate.

Blueberry Mold

First Layer:
1 (6 ounce) package lemon gelatin
1 cup boiling water
1 (8 ounce) package cream cheese, softened
3 tablespoons powdered sugar
1 (8 ounce) can crushed pineapple, undrained
1 cup half and half

Second Layer:
1 (6 ounce) package black-raspberry gelatin
1 cup boiling water
1 (15 ounce) can blueberries, drained
1 can blueberry pie filling

In your mixing bowl, dissolve lemon gelatin in boiling water, mixing well. Add cream cheese and powdered sugar and beat, slowly at first, until the mixture is smooth. Add the pineapple and the half and half and pour into a Pam sprayed 9 x 13 inch pan. Refrigerate until gelatin is firm. Dissolve the black-raspberry (you could also use black-cherry gelatin) in the boiling water. Stir in drained blueberries and the blueberry pie filling. Mix well Pour over the lemon gelatin mixture and refrigerate several hour before serving. Serve on a lettuce leaf and place the blueberry mixture on the bottom. Serves 12.

Cranberry Wiggle

1 (6 ounce) package cherry gelatin
1 cup boiling water
1 (16 ounce) can whole cranberry sauce
1 (15 ounce) can crushed pineapple, undrained
1 cup chopped apples
1 cup chopped pecans

Dissolve gelatin in boiling water; mixing well. Add cranberry sauce, pineapple, apples and pecans. Pour into a Pam sprayed 9 x 13 inch glass dish and refrigerate. Stir about the time it begins to set so the apples won't all stay on top. Serves 12.

Ambrosia Mold

2 envelopes unflavored gelatin
½ cup cold water
1 (20 ounce) can crushed pineapple
⅔ cup sugar
3 tablespoons lemon juice
1 (8 ounce) package cream cheese, softened
2 (11 ounce) cans mandarin oranges
⅔ cup chopped pecans
½ cup flaked coconut

In a cup, mix gelatin with the cold water. Drain the pineapple and add enough water to the juice to make 1 cup. Place juice in saucepan, heat to boiling point. Then add the gelatin mixture and stir until gelatin is dissolved. Remove from heat. Stir in sugar, lemon juice and cream cheese, using a wire whisk to blend. Chill to consistency of egg whites (about an hour in the refrigerator, but stir several times to check). Fold in pineapple, oranges, pecans and coconut. Serves 8. This is really a make-ahead ambrosia salad.

Emerald Salad

1 (3 ounce) package lime gelatin
¾ cup boiling water
1½ cucumbers, peeled and shredded (scoop seeds out)
2 teaspoons finely grated onion
1 tablespoon lemon juice
¼ teaspoon salt
1 cup mayonnaise
1 cup cream style small curd cottage cheese
1 (2.5 ounce) package slivered almonds, toasted

Dissolve gelatin in water and cool slightly. (Make sure you have at least 1 full cup of cucumbers.) Add cucumber, onion, lemon juice, salt, mayonnaise, cottage cheese and almonds. Pour into individual molds or into a 9 inch dish. Chill 8 hours. Serves 8.

I like this salad best when you can get fresh cucumbers from the garden (or Farmer's Market) and the best cucumbers are those long and "skinny" with very few seeds.

Buffet Egg Salad

9 hard-cooked eggs, divided
2 envelopes unflavored gelatin
½ cup cold water
1 cup mayonnaise
½ cup sour cream
2 tablespoons Dijon mustard
3 tablespoons lemon juice
1 (10 ounce) package frozen green peas, uncooked
1 (4 ounce) jar diced pimentos
3 stalks celery, thinly sliced
½ teaspoon salt
1 teaspoon seasoned salt
1 tablespoon dehydrated onion flakes
⅛ teaspoon cayenne pepper

Slice 2 eggs and mash 7. Sprinkle gelatin in the ½ cup water in a saucepan to soften. Heat over low heat, stirring constantly until gelatin is dissolved. Pour into a large bowl. Stir in the mayonnaise, sour cream, mustard, lemon juice and mashed eggs. Mix all together with whisk. Refrigerate until slightly thickened. Arrange the sliced eggs in the bottom of a greased 8 cup mold. When gelatin mixture is slightly thick, fold in green peas, pimentos, celery, salt, seasoned salt, onion flakes and cayenne pepper. Pour into the mold. Refrigerate.

Always wear black dresses to funerals, dresses to church and no white shoes until after Easter. — BCJ

Creamy Gazpacho Salad

1 can tomato soup
1 envelope plain gelatin
¼ cup cold water
1 (8-ounce) package cream cheese, softened
½ cup chopped celery
½ cup chopped bell pepper
1 tablespoon finely chopped onion
1 teaspoon lemon juice
½ cup chopped pecans
1 cup mayonnaise
⅓ cup sliced green olives

Heat soup, gelatin and water; blend. Add cream cheese and stir constantly while leaving on medium heat. Blend well. Cool and add remaining ingredients. Pour mixture into a mold or a 9 x 9inch Pyrex and let set overnight. Cut into squares to serve. Serves 8. To make a main dish, add 1 cup cooked shrimp.

This is delicious! Wonderful when you want a make-ahead salad - but not a sweet salad.

Molded Potato Salad

2 envelopes unflavored gelatin
1 cup buttermilk
8 cups cubed, cooked potatoes
6 hard-cooked eggs, diced
2 cups chopped celery
¾ cup chopped green onion, tops too
1 (2 ounce) jar pimiento
1 (8 ounce) carton sour cream
2 tablespoons sugar
1 tablespoon prepared mustard
1 tablespoon salt
¼ heaping teaspoon pepper
1 teaspoon seasoned salt

Oil a 12 cup bundt pan. In saucepan, combine gelatin and buttermilk. Heat over medium heat, stiffing until gelatin is dissolved. Cool. In large bowl, combine all ingredients and gelatin mixture. Heap the salad into the pan; press firmly into place. Cover and refrigerate until set. To unmold: use a thin, narrow knife and loosen center core of salad. Dip pan in hot water for about 10 seconds and turn out on serving plate. Garnish with celery leaves around edges of serving dish. Serves a bunch!

A mother understands
what a child never says.

— Jewish proverb

Molded Guacamole Ring

2 envelopes unflavored gelatin
½ cup cold water
1 cup boiling water
6 tablespoons lemon juice
¼ cup finely minced onion
4 fresh or canned tomatillos diced
2 teaspoons salt
Scant ⅛ teaspoon Tabasco
3½ cups mashed avocado
¾ cup mayonnaise
Cherry tomatoes or fresh tomatoes

Soften gelatin in cold water. Stir into boiling water. Add lemon juice, onion, 4 tomatoes, salt and Tabasco. Cool. Stir in avocado and mayonnaise. Pour into a 10 inch ring mold and chill until firm. To serve, place ring on a bed of lettuce with tomatoes in center of ring.

Artichoke Salad

1 envelope plain gelatin
¼ cup cold water
½ cup boiling water
1 cup mayonnaise (not salad dressing)
1 (14 ounce) can hearts of artichoke, well drained
½ (10 ounce) package frozen green peas, thawed, uncooked
2 tablespoons lemon juice
1 (4 ounce) jar chopped pimentos
1 bunch green onions, finely chopped, tops too
1½ cups shredded mozzarella cheese
1 teaspoon Italian herb seasoning
⅛ teaspoon cayenne pepper
½ teaspoon garlic powder
Paprika

Soften gelatin in cold water. Add boiling water and mix well. Add mayonnaise and stir until smooth. Remove any spikes or tough leaves from artichoke hearts and chop. Add all remaining ingredients except paprika. Pour into a ring mold and refrigerate. When ready to serve, slip knife around edges to loosen from mold. Unmold onto a serving plate lined with lettuce. Sprinkle paprika over salad. You could put radishes, olives or black olives, in center of mold when serving.

When one is too nice, he/she usually wants something. — BCJ

Wagon Wheels

3 hard cooked eggs
1 (3 ounce) package cream cheese, softened
1 cup grated Monterey Jack cheese
⅓ cup very finely chopped celery
Several shakes Tabasco
⅓ cup finely chopped pecans
¼ cup mayonnaise
1 teaspoon prepared mustard
¼ teaspoon salt
¼ teaspoon white pepper
3 medium green peppers
Lettuce leaves

Mash eggs and mix well with cream cheese and Monterey Jack cheese. Add celery, Tabasco, pecans, mayonnaise, mustard, salt and white pepper. Mix well. Cut off tops of green peppers and remove seeds and membranes. Stuff with the cheese mixture. Chill several hours or preferably overnight. Cut peppers in ¼ inch rings. For each serving, overlap pepper slices on a lettuce leaf. Serves 6 to 8.

My mother said to me, 'If you become a soldier, you'll be a general; if you become a monk, you'll end up as pope. Instead, I became a painter and wound up as a Picasso.

— Pablo Picasso

Cauliflower and Broccoli Salad

1 (8 ounce) carton sour cream
1 cup mayonnaise
1 package original Ranch dressing mix
1 large head cauliflower, broken into bite size pieces
1 large bunch fresh broccoli, broken into bite size pieces
1 (10 ounce) box frozen green peas, thawed, uncooked
3 stalks celery, sliced
1 bunch green onions, chopped, tops too
1 (8 ounce) can water chestnuts, drained
⅓ cup sweet relish, drained
8 ounces mozzarella cheese, cut in chunks
2 (2.25 ounce) packages slivered almonds, toasted

Mix together the sour cream, mayonnaise and dressing mix; set aside. MAKE SURE cauliflower and broccoli are WELL DRAINED. In a large container mix together all salad ingredients. Add dressing and toss. Refrigerate. Serves 12.

This is one of my most favorite salads. It goes well with just about everything.

Raisin-Broccoli Salad

1 bunch fresh broccoli, cut in small bite-sized florets
½ purple onion, sliced and separated
½ cup raisins
1 package slivered almonds
½ cup chopped celery
Imitation bacon bits
Dressing:
1 cup mayonnaise
¼ cup sugar
2 tablespoons vinegar
1 teaspoon salt
½ teaspoon pepper

Make sure broccoli has been well drained. In a large bowl, combine broccoli, onion, raisins, almonds and celery. Mix together dressing ingredients and pour over vegetables; toss. Refrigerate several hours before serving. Sprinkle bacon bits over salad just before serving. Serves 6 to 8.

When I first saw this salad – I thought, "Raisins in my salad – no way! But I was wrong. This is my favorite broccoli salad – and now we know how good broccoli is for us!

Marinated Brussel Sprouts

2 (10 ounce) packages frozen Brussel sprouts
½ cup oil
½ cup tarragon vinegar
2 tablespoons sugar
1 clove garlic, crushed
1 teaspoon salt
½ teaspoon seasoned salt
1 teaspoon pepper
2 small onions, cut in rings

Cook Brussel sprouts according to instructions on package. *For quicker cooking, you can pierce the boxes several times and cook in the microwave on high for 6 to 7 minutes for each box. In a medium size container with a lid, mix the oil, vinegar, sugar, garlic, salt, seasoned salt and pepper. Add Brussel sprouts and onion rings to the dressing. Put lid on container and shake well. Refrigerate at least 24 hours before serving.

Most mothers are
instinctive philosophers.
—Harriet Beacher Stowe

Black-Eyed Pea Salad

2 (16 ounce) cans Jalapeno black-eyed peas, drained
1 ripe avocado, peeled and chopped
½ purple onion, chopped
1 cup chopped celery
1 bell Pepper, chopped

Dressing:
⅓ cup oil
⅓ cup white vinegar
3 tablespoons sugar
¼ teaspoon garlic powder
½ teaspoon salt

In a large bowl, mix all salad ingredients together. Mix dressing ingredients together. Add dressing to vegetables and toss. Refrigerate. Serves 10.

Marinated Black-Eyed Pea Salad

2 cans jalapeno black-eyed peas, rinsed, drained
1 cup chopped celery
1 (4 ounce) can chopped green chilies
½ purple onion, chopped
2 tablespoons fresh cilantro*
2 cloves garlic, crushed
1 teaspoon seasoned salt
½ teaspoon black pepper
1 teaspoon Worcestershire
1½ cups Italian dressing
2 hard boiled eggs, sliced
3 fresh green onions, chopped, tops too

(Continued on Next

(Continued)

In a large bowl, with a lid, combine all ingredients except eggs and green onions. Add the dressing and stir to mix well. If liquid doesn't cover peas, add a little more dressing. Marinate, covered for 24 hours in refrigerator. When ready to serve, use a slotted spoon and place salad in a crystal bowl. Sprinkle with sliced eggs and green onions. Serves 8 to 10. *You can substitute 2 teaspoons dried- cilantro.

Summer Cucumber Crisps

1 pint white vinegar

1½ cups sugar

1 clove garlic, chopped

1 tablespoon whole cloves

1 tablespoon whole allspice

2 bay leaves

2 sticks cinnamon

1 tablespoon whole celery seed

1 tablespoon mustard seed

1 tablespoon peppercorns

1 teaspoon powdered ginger

5 to 6 cucumbers, preferably fresh from the garden

In a medium saucepan combine all ingredients except the cucumbers. Boil 12 to 15 minutes. Cool mixture and strain. Thinly slice the cucumbers and place in a large jar or bowl with a lid. Add cooled marinade and cover tightly. Keep refrigerated.

Crunchy Pea Salad

1 (16 ounce) package frozen English peas, thawed, not cooked
½ head small cauliflower, cut into small florets
1 cup chopped celery
1 (8 ounce) can water chestnuts, drained
1 (2 ounce) jar pimentos, drained
1½ cups mayonnaise
¼ cup Italian dressing
½ teaspoon salt
½ teaspoon seasoned salt
A scant ⅛ teaspoon cayenne pepper
1 cup peanuts
½ cup bacon bits

In a bowl with a cover, combine all ingredients except the peanuts and bacon bits; toss well. Refrigerate. When ready to serve, add the peanuts and bacon bits, toss. Cover. Serves 8 to 10.

Winte

1 (16 ounce) can French st
1 (16 ounce) can jalapeno bl
1 (16 ounce) can shoe peg w
1 (16 ounce) can English p
1 (2 ounce) jar chopped p
1 bell pepper, chopped
1 onion, sliced and broken into

Dressing:
¾ cup sugar
1 teaspoon salt
1 teaspoon seasoned salt
½ teaspoon garlic powder
1 teaspoon seasoned pepper
½ cup oil
¾ cup vinegar

In a 3 quart container with lid, combine dressing ingredients; mix. Add all drained vegetables to container and stir. Cover and refrigerate. Serves 16.

I keep a supply of these ingredients on hand — and when you need to take a dish to a friend — it's a salad in a hurry!

Calico Salad

1 (16 ounce) can green beans
1 (16 ounce) can peas
1 (16 ounce) can whole kernel white corn
1 cup finely chopped celery
1 green pepper, chopped
1 bunch green onions, chopped
1 (2 ounce) jar chopped pimento, drained

Dressing:
½ cup sugar
½ cup wine vinegar
½ cup oil
1 teaspoon salt
½ teaspoon pepper
½ teaspoon tarragon
½ teaspoon basil

Drain all vegetables and combine in a bowl that has a lid. Mix dressing ingredients thoroughly and pour over vegetables. Cover and refrigerate overnight. Will keep several days in refrigerator. Serves 8 to 10.

Beauty is as Beauty does. — BCJ

Savory Spinach Salad

½ cup oil
½ cup red wine vinegar
3 tablespoons catsup
¼ cup sugar
1 teaspoon salt
½ teaspoon garlic powder
½ teaspoon dry mustard
Pepper
1 (10-ounce) package fresh spinach
4 hard-cooked eggs, sliced
8 slices bacon, crisply cooked and crumbled
1 cup fresh mushrooms, sliced
1 red onion, thinly sliced
1 (8-ounce) can sliced water chestnuts, optional
Croutons

Combine first 8 ingredients to make dressing. Refrigerate at least 6 hours before serving. Wash, drain and tear spinach into bite-size pieces. When ready to serve, toss spinach with eggs, bacon, mushrooms, onion and water chestnuts and then the dressing. Top with croutons. Serves 8.

Spinach and Strawberry Salad

2 (10 ounce) packages of fresh spinach
1 quart fresh strawberries, halved
½ cup slivered almonds, toasted

Poppy Seed Dressing:
⅓ cup sugar
¼ cup apple cider vinegar
½ teaspoon dried onion flakes
¼ teaspoon paprika
½ teaspoon white wine Worcestershire
½ cup oil
1 tablespoon poppy seeds

Wash and remove spinach from the spinach leaves. Tear into smaller pieces and add the strawberries and almonds. Refrigerate until ready to serve. To make dressing, combine sugar, vinegar, onion flakes, paprika and Worcestershire in a blender. Process 15 to 20 seconds. Add the oil and process another 15 seconds. Stir in poppy seeds. When ready to serve, pour dressing over chilled spinach salad.

It's ok if you lose today.
You'll win tomorrow. — BCJ

Orange-Almond Greens

⅓ cup slivered almonds, toasted
2 (11 ounce) cans mandarin oranges, drained
1 bunch green onions, chopped, tops too
2 heads romaine lettuce, torn in small pieces
1 cup packaged croutons

Dressing:
¼ cup sugar
1 teaspoon dry mustard
1 teaspoon salt
¼ cup cider vinegar
½ cup salad oil
2 tablespoons poppy seeds

Toast the almonds for 15 minutes in a 275 degree oven. Combine the oranges, onion and lettuce. Mix all dressing ingredients together. Just before serving, add the croutons to the lettuce mixture and pour only the amount of dressing needed (stir the dressing well just before adding to salad). Serves 6.

You can do anything if you want
it bad enough. — BCJ

Bow Tie Salad

Dressing:
1¼ cups mayonnaise
⅓ cup freshly grated Parmesan cheese
⅓ cup chopped fresh parsley
¼ teaspoon oregano
¼ teaspoon basil
¾ teaspoon garlic powder
½ teaspoon salt

Salad:
4 ounces bow tie pasta, cooked and drained
4 ounces salami, cut into small cubes
1 (8 ounce) can artichoke hearts, drained and quartered
1½ cups thinly sliced zucchini
1½ cups broccoli flowerets
½ cup diced red pepper
½ cup pine nuts, toasted

Mix dressing ingredients together in a large bowl. Add all the salad ingredients to the bowl and toss well. Cover and refrigerate for at least 2 hours before serving. Serves 8 to 10.

Mothers never get time and a half.

— Anonymous

130

Crunchy Chinese Slaw

1 head green cabbage, grated
½ head red cabbage, grated
1 cup slivered almonds, toasted
1 bunch green onions, sliced
1 large green bell pepper, diced
1 cup sliced celery
1 (11 ounce) can Mandarin oranges, drained
2 packages chicken-flavored Ramen
noodles, crumbled (uncooked)
1 cup suflower seeds

Dressing:
1 cup oil
¾ tarragon vinegar
¾ cup sugar
2 teaspoons salt
1 teaspoon pepper
¾ teaspoon seasoned salt
2 dashes Tabasco (optional)

(I splurge on the cabbage. I buy 2 heads of green cabbage and use only the outer greenest leaves – an amount equal to one head of green cabbage. I also cut only the outer red leaves of the red cabbage.) Toast the almonds for 15 minutes at 275 degrees while grating the cabbage. In a large bowl, mix together all dressing ingredients and pour over cabbage mixture; toss well. This will serve an army (about 18)! And you can make it the day before serving!

Layered Company Salad

1 package fresh spinach, torn into pieces
1 cup sliced fresh mushrooms
1 bunch green onions, chopped, tops too
1 (10 ounce) package frozen green peas, uncooked
3 ribs celery, sliced (optional)
1½ cups grated Cheddar cheese
2 teaspoons sugar, divided
Salt
Pepper
4 hard-boiled eggs, grated
1 bell pepper, chopped
1 cucumber, sliced (optional)
½ head cauliflower, chopped
1 cup grated Monterey Jack cheese

Dressing:
1½ cups mayonnaise
1½ cups sour cream

You will need a very large crystal bowl for this salad (about 10 inches in diameter). Place a layer (one-half) of spinach. Next the mushrooms, green onions, frozen peas, celery and ½ of the Cheddar cheese. In a bowl, combine mayonnaise and sour cream and spread ½ over top of cheese. Sprinkle with 1 teaspoon sugar, salt and lots of pepper. Next layer remaining spinach, eggs, bell pepper, cucumber, cauliflower and remaining Cheddar cheese. Spread remaining dressing on top. Sprinkle 1 teaspoon sugar, salt and pepper. Top with Monterey Jack cheese. Cover with plastic wrap and refrigerate overnight. Serves 15.

Potato Salad Reunion

7 medium potatoes, cooked in jackets, peeled and sliced
⅓ cup Italian dressing
¾ cup sliced green onions,m tops too.
3 hard-boiled eggs, chopped
1 cup chopped celery
1 (2-ounce) jar chopped pimentos
½ cup pickle relish, drained
1 cup mayonnaise
½ cup sour cream
1 tablespoon prepared mustard
1 teaspoon seasoned salt
1 teaspoon seasoned pepper
½ teaspoon salt
½ teaspoon
Creole seasoning
1 teaspoon sugar
Paprika

Boil potatoes until tender. While still warm, peel, slice and pour dressing over potatoes. Chill several hours. Add onions, eggs, celery, pimento and pickle relish and toss. Then add mayonnaise, sour cream, mustard and seasonings, except paprika and fold into potato mixture. Refrigerate. Place in a crystal bowl and garnish with paprika. Serves 12 to 14.

Cornbread Salad

2 (6 ounce) packages Mexican cornbread mix
2 eggs
1⅓ cups milk
2 ribs celery, sliced
1 bunch green onions, chopped (tops too)
1 green bell pepper, chopped
2 firm tomatoes, chopped and drained
8 slices bacon, cooked and cut-up
1 cup grated Cheddar cheese
1 (8 ounce) can whole kernel corn, drained
½ cup ripe olives, chopped (optional)
2½ cups mayonnaise

Prepare cornbread as directed with the eggs and milk. Cook, cool and crumble cornbread in a large mixing bowl. Add the celery, green onions, bell pepper, tomatoes, bacon, cheese, corn, olives and mayonnaise. Mix well. Serves 16.

Sunflower Salad

2 medium apples, cored and chopped
¾ cup seedless green grapes, halved
½ cup chopped celery
½ cup chopped pecans
½ cup sunflower seeds
⅓ cup mayonnaise
1 banana, sliced
Lettuce leaves

In a medium size mixing bowl, toss together apples, grapes, celery, pecans and sunflower seeds. Fold in mayonnaise and banana. Serve on individual lettuce lined salad plates. It may also be served in a pretty crystal bowl. Serves 6.

Almond Chicken Salad

4 cups cooked, chopped chicken breasts
1½ cups chopped celery
½ apple, peeled, diced
1 (8 ounce) can crushed pineapple, well drained
1 cup toasted slivered almonds
1 cup red grapes, cut in half
1 ½ teaspoons salt
1 teaspoon dry mustard
¼ teaspoon pepper
3 tablespoons lemon juice
¼ cup sour cream
1 cup mayonnaise

In a large mixing bowl, combine chicken, celery, apple, pineapple, almonds and grapes. Add salt, mustard, pepper, lemon juice, sour cream and mayonnaise and toss. Refrigerate. Serves 8.

Crunchy Chicken Salad

4½ cups cooked, chopped chicken breasts
1 (8 ounce) can water chestnuts
1 cup chopped celery
1 cup green grapes, sliced in half
1 (2.25 ounce) package sliced almonds

Dressing:
1 (3 ounce) package cream cheese, softened
1 cup mayonnaise
1 tablespoon lemon juice
1 tablespoon Grey Poupon Dijon mustard
½ teaspoon black pepper
1 teaspoon salt
Lettuce

In a large bowl, combine chicken, water chestnuts, celery, grapes and almonds. In a smaller bowl, combine cream cheese and mayonnaise and mix with a fork until the cream cheese is smooth. To the cream cheese and mayonnaise mixture, add the lemon juice, mustard, pepper and salt. Fold the dressing into the chicken mixture. Serve on a bed of lettuce. Refrigerate. Serves 8.

Keep your priorities straight. — BCJ

136

Cranberry-Chicken Salad

Layer 1:
1½ envelopes unflavored gelatin
¼ cup cold water
1 (16 ounce) can whole cranberry sauce
1 (8 ounce) can crushed pineapple
¼ cup sugar
1 cup chopped pecans
Red food coloring (optional)

Layer 2:
1½ envelopes unflavored gelatin
¼ cup cold water
½ cup water
1 (3 ounce) package cream cheese
3 tablespoons lemon juice
¾ teaspoon salt
2 cups diced cooked chicken
¾ cup chopped celery
¼ cup sweet relish
1 cup chopped pecans

LAYER 1: Soften gelatin in cold water. Place cranberry sauce, pineapple and sugar in sauce pan. Heat to boiling point. Add gelatin mixture and stir well. Mix in pecans and red food coloring. Pour into a Pam sprayed 9 x 13 inch glass dish and chill.

LAYER 2: Soften gelatin in ¼ cup cold water. Place ½ cup water, cream cheese, lemon juice and salt in sauce pan. Bring to a boll and stir until cream cheese is dissolved. Stir in gelatin mixture. Fold in chicken, celery, relish and pecans. Pour on top of cranberry mixture. Chill. To serve, cut into squares and put cranberry side up on a bed of lettuce.

This is great for a holiday luncheon. It's really good with the Almond Asparagus Bake on page 148 and the White Chocolate Cheesecake on page 266 as the grand finale.

Southwestern Chicken Salad

4 cups cubed, cooked chicken breast
1 (16 ounce) can black beans, drained
¾ red onion, chopped
½ red bell pepper, chopped
½ yellow bell pepper, chopped
¼ cup chopped fresh cilantro
½ cup sour cream
¼ cup mayonnaise
½ teaspoon garlic powder
1 jalapeno pepper, finely chopped
1 teaspoon lime juice
1 teaspoon salt
½ teaspoon pepper
½ cup toasted pine nuts

Combine chicken, beans, onion, bell peppers and cilantro in a large bowl. In a small bowl, whisk sour cream and mayonnaise together. Stir in garlic powder, jalapeno pepper and lime juice. Add to large bowl of chicken. Add salt and pepper; toss. Refrigerate at least an hour before serving. Just before serving, toss in pine nuts. Serve on a bed of lettuce. Serves 8.

Hawaiian Chicken Salad

1 cup cooked rice
3½ cups cooked, cubed chicken breasts
2 cups diced celery
1 (8 ounce) can water chestnuts, drained and chopped
1 (15 ounce) cans pineapple tidbits, well drained
1 (3½ ounce) can coconut
1 banana, sliced

Dressing:
1¾ to 2 cups mayonnaise
2 scant tablespoons lemon juice
¼ teaspoon salt
½ teaspoon white pepper
1 teaspoon curry powder

Combine all ingredients in a large mixing bowl. Combine dressing ingredients and fold into chicken salad. Chill several hours before serving. Serves 10. Really delicious!

Tropical Chicken Salad in Red Cabbage Leaves

6 chicken breasts, cooked and cubed

2 mangoes, peeled and cubed

2 cups fresh pineapple, cubed

1 cup seedless green grapes

2 scallions, white only, minced

¾ cup slivered almonds, toasted

1 tablespoon fresh minced ginger
(or ¼ teaspoon ground ginger)

1 tablespoon fresh minced cilantro
(or ¼ teaspoon ground cilantro)

1 teaspoon salt

½ teaspoon white pepper

¼ teaspoon nutmeg

2 tablespoons lime juice

¾ cup mayonnaise

½ cup sour cream

8 large red cabbage leaves

Orange slices for garnish

Combine chicken, mangoes, pineapple, grapes, scallions, almonds, ginger, cilantro, salt, white pepper and nutmeg in a large mixing bowl. Toss lightly. Sprinkle lime juice over top and toss. In a small bowl, combine mayonnaise and sour cream. Pour dressing over salad and toss gently to coat. Place one cabbage leaf on each plate and mound salad in each leaf. Garnish each plate with a peeled orange slice.

This is a beautiful course for a luncheon. When you serve it with the Vegetable Frittata on page 173, the Lime Mint Salad on page 100 and the quick and easy Crunchy Bread Sticks on page 45, people will rave. I promise!

Chicken Salad Squares

5 chicken breasts, cooked and finely chopped
2 tablespoons plain gelatin
½ cup water
1 (14½ ounce) can chicken broth
1 (8 ounce) package cream cheese, softened
1 cup mayonnaise
1 (4 ounce) jar pimento, drained
1 cup slivered almonds, toasted
3 tablespoons capers
3 hard cooked eggs, chopped
1½ cups chopped celery
½ teaspoon salt
½ teaspoon white pepper

Mix gelatin with water and set aside. Bring broth to a boil and dissolve in hot broth. Remove from heat. With mixer, beat together cream cheese and mayonnaise until creamy. Fold in chicken. Pimento, almonds, capers, eggs, celery, salt and white pepper. Pour into a Pam sprayed 9 x 13 inch dish. Refrigerate several hours before cutting in squares. Serve on a lettuce leaf. (You can use canned chicken, drained instead of chicken breasts. You will need 2 (12 ounce) cans. Serves 8 to 10.

Molded Tuna Salad

3 envelopes plain gelatin
½ cup cold water
1 can cream of chicken soup
2 cans tuna, rinsed
1 cup mayonnaise
1 cup chopped celery
3 boiled eggs, chopped
1½ teaspoons Worcestershire
½ cup chopped stuffed olives

Mix gelatin and water and let dissolve. In a medium saucepan, heat the soup and stir in gelatin; mix well and set aside. In a mixing bowl, combine tuna, mayonnaise, celery, eggs, Worcestershire and olives; mix. Add soup mixture and pour into Pam greased mold or a greased 8 x 12 inch glass dish.

*This is really an "old-time" recipe, but still one of my favorites.
It is a wonderful luncheon treat!*

Crunchy Tuna Salad

2 (7 ounce) cans white tuna in water, drained
¼ cup chopped onion
½ cup chopped celery
¼ cup chopped ripe olives
1 (2 ounce) jar chopped pimentos
⅔ cup mayonnaise
1 tablespoon wine vinegar
1 (3 ounce) can chow mein noodles

In a mixing bowl, combine all ingredients except noodles and refrigerate. Just before serving, toss with noodles. Serves 6.

Shrimp Mousse

1 can tomato soup
2 envelopes plain gelatin
⅓ cup cold water
1 (8 ounce) package cream cheese, softened
½ cup chopped celery
½ cup chopped bell pepper
2 tablespoons finely chopped onion
1 teaspoon lemon juice
½ cup chopped pecans
1 cup mayonnaise
⅓ cup sliced green olives (optional)
1 teaspoon Worcestershire sauce
2 (4 ounce) cans deveined shrimp

Heat soup, gelatin and water; blend. Add cream cheese and stir constantly while leaving on low heat and until cream cheese has melted. Blend well. Cool and add remaining ingredients. Pour mixture into shell or a fish mold. Refrigerate overnight. Serve with crackers. This could also be served at a luncheon. Serves 8.

You must do the thing you
think you cannot do.
— Eleanor Roosevelt

Shrimp and English Pea Salad

2 cups frozen shrimp, cooked and cleaned
1 (10 ounce) package frozen green peas, thawed (uncooked)
2 stalks celery, chopped
1 cup mayonnaise
⅓ cup India relish, drained
1 tablespoon lemon juice
½ teaspoon curry powder
½ teaspoon pepper
¼ teaspoon salt
1 (3 ounce) can chow mein noodles
1 cup chopped cashews
Lettuce leaves

With paper towels, blot shrimp well making sure all liquid is gone. Combine all ingredients except noodles, cashews and lettuce in a large bowl and mix well. Cover and refrigerate at least an hour. Just before serving, add noodles and cashews; toss. Serve on lettuce leaves. Serves 8.

Simply Scrumptious Shrimp Sa

3 cups cooked shrimp, chopped
1 cup chopped celery
4 hard-boiled eggs, chopped
½ cup sliced green stuffed olives, well drained
¼ cup sliced green onions
¼ cup chopped dill pickle
1 cup mayonnaise
2 tablespoons chili sauce
1 tablespoon horseradish
1 teaspoon seasoned salt
¾ teaspoon seasoned pepper

Combine all ingredients and toss lightly. Refrigerate. Serves 6 to 8.

Shrimp Monterey Salad

1 pound cooked tiny shrimp
2 tablespoon fresh grated Parmesan cheese
¼ cup oil
3 tablespoons red wine vinegar
1 tablespoon lemon juice
2 teaspoons Dijon mustard
½ teaspoon black pepper
½ teaspoon salt
3 medium avocados, peeled and halved
1½ cups grated Monterey Jack cheese

Combine shrimp and Parmesan cheese in a bowl with a lid. Mix together the oil, vinegar, lemon juice, mustard, pepper and salt. Pour dressing over shrimp and marinate 2 hours. Place 1 avocado half in each of 6 individual ramekins. Divide seafood evenly onto the avocados halves. Sprinkle with Monterey Jack cheese. Serve immediately.

Shrimp Remoulade

½ cup mayonnaise
¼ cup prepared horseradish
2 tablespoons
Grey Poupon mustard
¼ cup oil
½ cup chili sauce
2 teaspoons lemon juice
¼ teaspoon cayenne pepper
1 teaspoon paprika
½ teaspoon garlic powder
1 tablespoon chopped capers
½ bunch green onions, very finely chopped
1 pound cooked, shelled, deveined shrimp
Lettuce
3 hard boiled eggs, sliced

Combine all ingredients except shrimp, lettuce and eggs; mix well. On each of 6 small individual plates; place lettuce leaves. Place shrimp on top and spoon on the sauce. Garnish each dish with egg wedges.

Eat your vegetables.

Almond Asparagus Bake

5 (10 ounce) cans asparagus
1½ cups cracker crumbs
4 eggs, hard-boiled and sliced
1½ cups grated Cheddar cheese
1 stick margarine, melted
½ cup milk
2 (2-5 ounce) packages sliced almonds

Drain asparagus and arrange half the asparagus in a Pam sprayed 9 x 13 inch baking dish. Cover with ¾ cup crumbs and half the sliced eggs; sprinkle with ½ of the cheese. Layer remaining asparagus, ¾ cup crumbs and remaining eggs. Drizzle margarine and milk over casserole and top with almonds and the remaining cheese. Bake at 350 degrees for 30 minutes. Serves 10 to 12.

Asparagus Cheese Bake

2 (15 ounce) cans cut asparagus spears, reserve liquid
3 hard-cooked eggs, chopped
½ cup chopped pecans
1 can cream of asparagus soup
½ stick margarine
½ teaspoon black pepper
2 cups cracker crumbs
2 cups Monterey Jack cheese, grated

Arrange the drained asparagus spears in a buttered 2 quart casserole dish. Top with chopped eggs and pecans. Heat asparagus soup, liquid from the can of asparagus, margarine and pepper. Pour over asparagus, eggs and pecans. Combine cracker crumbs and cheese. Sprinkle over casserole. Bake at 350 degrees for 25 minutes. Serves 8.

Better Butter Beans

1 cup sliced celery
1 cup chopped onion
½ stick margarine
1 (10 ounce) can diced tomatoes and green chilies
¾ teaspoon salt
½ teaspoon sugar
½ teaspoon pepper
2 (17-ounce) cans butter beans

Sauté celery and onion in margarine for about 3 minutes. Add tomatoes and chilies, salt, sugar and pepper. Add butter beans; cover and simmer 25 to 30 minutes. Serves 8.

Baked Beans

EASY

2 (16 ounce) cans pork and beans, slightly drained
1 tablespoon Worcestershire
½ onion, chopped
⅔ cup packed brown sugar
3 dashes Tabasco
1 teaspoon prepared mustard
1¼ cup catsup
3 strips bacon

In a mixing bowl, combine beans, Worcestershire, onion, Sugar, Tabasco, mustard and catsup and mix well. Pour into a greased casserole and place bacon strips over beans and bake at 350 degrees for 45 to 50 Minutes. Serves 8.

Frijoles Ole'

3 cups dry pinto beans, washed
5 quarts boiling water
2 tablespoons chili powder
1 jalapeno pepper, cut into wedges
¼ cup chopped onion
2 teaspoons garlic powder
½ teaspoon ground cumin
2 tablespoons cilantro
3 tablespoons catsup
¼ stick margarine
1 tablespoon salt

Place beans in an 8 quart saucepan; pour boiling water over beans and soak overnight Cook on high heat uncovered for about 30 minutes. Lower heat and add all ingredients except salt; cover and Simmer for about 2-1/2 to 3 hours or until beans are soft, but not mushy. Add salt. Serves 14 to 16.

Pine Nut Green Beans

1 (16 ounce) package frozen green beans
½ stick margarine
¾ cup pine nuts
¼ teaspoon garlic powder
½ teaspoon salt
½ teaspoon black pepper
½ teaspoon celery salt

Cook beans in water in a covered 3 quart saucepan for 10 to 15 minutes or until tender-crisp; drain. Melt margarine in skillet over medium heat and add pine nuts. Cook, stirring frequently until golden. Add pine nuts to the green beans and season with the garlic powder, salt, black pepper and celery salt. Serves 8.

Green Bean Supreme

¼ stick margarine
1 (10 ounce) can cream of mushroom soup
1 (3 ounce) package cream cheese, softened
3 (16 ounce) cans French style green beans, drained
1 tablespoon dried onion flakes
1 (8 ounce) can sliced water chestnuts, drained
½ teaspoon garlic powder
½ teaspoon seasoned salt
1½ cups grated Cheddar cheese
1 cup cracker crumbs
1 (2 ounce) package slivered almonds

Melt margarine in a large saucepan and add soup and cream cheese. Cook over low heat, stirring constantly just until cream cheese is melted and mixture is fairly smooth. Remove from heat and stir in green beans, onion flakes, water chestnuts, garlic powder, seasoned salt and cheese. Mix well. Pour into a Pam sprayed 9 x 13 inch casserole dish. Top with cracker crumbs and then almonds. Bake uncovered at 350 degrees for 30 minutes or until casserole bubbles around edges. Serves 8.

Green Bean Olé

3 cans French cut green beans
1 cup sour cream
8 ounces jalapeno Velveeta cheese, cut in chunks
½ onion, minced
½ teaspoon pepper
2 cups crushed Rice Krispies*
3 tablespoons margarine, melted

Drain green beans well. Butter a 2 ½ quart baking dish. In a large saucepan, melt the sour cream and jalapeno Velveeta cheese, stirring constantly. Add onion, pepper and green beans, mix. Pour into the buttered baking dish. Combine crushed Rice Krispies; and margarine and sprinkle over green bean mixture and bake at 350 degrees for 30 minutes. Serves 8 to 10. (Corn flakes will work well too.)

Broccoli Rice Whiz

1¼ cups rice, uncooked
¾ cup chopped onion
¾ cup chopped bell pepper
¾ cup chopped celery
½ stick margarine
1 (8-ounce) hot Mexican Cheese Whiz
1 can cream of chicken soup
½ cup milk
1 (16-ounce) package frozen chopped broccoli

Cook rice by package directions in a large saucepan and drain. Sauté onions, bell pepper and celery in margarine. Add onion, bell pepper and celery to the rice while still hot. Fold in Cheese Whiz, chicken soup and milk and mix. Heat on low burner just

(Continued on Next Page)

(Continued)

until cheese and soup are well blended. Fold in chopped broccoli. Pour into a large greased casserole and bake 30 to 35 minutes at 350 degrees. Serves 12. Can be made a day early and baked the next day.

Broccoli Soufflé

4 cups fresh broccoli flowerets
2 tablespoons water
5 tablespoons margarine, melted
2 tablespoons flour
3 eggs, slightly beaten
8 ounces small curd cottage cheese
½ cup half and half
1 cup grated Cheddar cheese
½ cup minced onion
¼ teaspoon salt
½ teaspoon seasoned salt
½ teaspoon white pepper

When cutting broccoli, leave very little of the stem on the broccoli. In microwaveable bowl, place flowerets and water. Microwave on high for 3 minutes. Remove from microwave oven, add margarine and sprinkle the flour over broccoli; toss. In the bowl you have beaten the eggs, add the cottage cheese, half and half, ½ cup cheese, onion, salt, seasoned salt and white pepper. Mix together well. Combine the broccoli and the egg mixture and pour into a Pam sprayed 7 x 11 inch glass dish. Sprinkle the remaining ½ cup cheese over the top. Bake at 350 degrees for 30 to 35 minutes; until center is set. If you want to make this ahead of time, cook only 25 minutes, refrigerate. To finish cooking, let casserole get to room temperature and cook an additional 15 minutes; the sides will be bubbly. Serves 6 to 8.

Broccoli and Cauliflower Casserole

1 (10 ounce) package frozen broccoli spears
1 (10 ounce) package frozen cauliflower
1 egg
²/₃ cup mayonnaise
1 can cream of chicken soup, undiluted
1 cup grated Swiss cheese
1 onion, chopped
1 cup breadcrumbs
¼ stick margarine
Paprika

Cook broccoli and cauliflower as directed on packages. Drain well and place in large mixing bowl. In a saucepan, combine egg, mayonnaise and soup and heat. Pour over vegetables; add cheese and onion and mix well. Pour into a 9 x 13 buttered baking dish. Combine breadcrumbs and margarine and sprinkle over broccoli and cauliflower mixture. Sprinkle paprika over top. Bake at 350 degrees for 30 to 35 minutes. Serves 8 to 10.

Impossible Broccoli Pie

1 (16 ounce) package frozen broccoli spears, thawed
12 ounces grated Cheddar cheese, divided
²/₃ cup chopped onion
3 eggs
¾ cup buttermilk biscuit mix
1½ cups milk
¾ teaspoon salt
¾ teaspoon pepper

Cut large chunks of the broccoli into smaller pieces. In a large

(Continued on Next Page)

(Continued)

mixing bowl, combine broccoli, ⅔ of the cheese and onion; mix. Pour into a greased 10 inch deep-dish pie plate. In the same mixing bowl, mix eggs and biscuit mix; beat for a couple of minutes. Add milk, salt and pepper and mix until fairly smooth. Pour over broccoli and cheese mixture. Bake at 375 degrees for 35 to 40 minutes or until knife inserted in center comes out clean. Top with remaining cheese and bake just until cheese is melted. Let stand 5 minute before serving. Serves 6 to 8.

Cauliflower Medley

1 large head cauliflower
1 (16 ounce) can Italian recipe stewed tomatoes
1 onion, finely chopped
1 green bell pepper, diced
1 tablespoon sugar
1 teaspoon salt
½ teaspoon black pepper
1 tablespoon cornstarch
½ stick margarine, melted
1 cup grated Cheddar cheese
¾ cup crackers or dry breadcrumbs

Break cauliflower into pieces and cook in a large saucepan with salted water for about 10 minutes (tender crisp). Drain well. Add the stewed tomatoes, onion, bell pepper, sugar, salt, black pepper, cornstarch and melted margarine. Transfer mixture to a 2 quart casserole dish and sprinkle cheese over top. Sprinkle with crumbs. Bake in a preheated 350 degree oven for 35 minutes. Serves 8.

I took this to our church supper one time and everybody loved the combination of cauliflower and tomato!

Cauliflower Con Queso

1 large head cauliflower, broken into flowerets
½ stick margarine
½ onion, chopped
2 tablespoons flour
1 (16 ounce) cans Mexican stewed tomatoes
1 (4 ounce) can chopped green chilies, drained
¾ teaspoon seasoned pepper
1 teaspoon salt
1½ cups grated Monterey Jack cheese

Cook flowerets until just crisp-tender. Drain and set aside. Melt margarine in medium saucepan. Add onion and cook just until clear. Blend in flour, then stir in tomatoes. Cook, stirring constantly until mixture thickens. Add green chilies, seasoned pepper and salt. Fold in cheese and stir until melted. Pour sauce over drained hot cauliflower and serve. (If you don't want that "Zippy hot" taste, use just plain stewed tomatoes.) Serves 6 to 8.

If you want to cook the cauliflower earlier, place it in a your serving dish and microwave the cauliflower about 15 seconds, just enough to warm. Then pour tomato-cheese mixture over the cauliflower.

Classic Cauliflower

2 (10 ounce) packages frozen cauliflower
4 slices bacon
1 can cream of chicken soup
1 cup cracker crumbs, divided
½ cup sour cream
1 (2 ounce) jar chopped pimentos
½ cup grated Cheddar cheese

Cook cauliflower according to package directions, just until

(Continued on Next Page)

(Continued)

tender. Drain and place in a medium sized, greased baking dish. Fry bacon crisp and crumble, set aside. In a medium saucepan, mix soup, ½ cup crumbs, sour cream, pimentos and cheese. Heat just until all ingredients are well mixed. Pour over cauliflower and top with remaining crumbs. Bake at 350 degrees for 20 to 25 minutes. Sprinkle crumbled bacon over casserole before serving.

Baked Cauliflower

1 (16 ounce) package frozen cauliflower
1 egg
⅔ cup mayonnaise
1 (10 ounce) can cream of chicken soup
4 ounces Swiss cheese, grated
2 ribs celery, sliced
1 bell pepper, seeded and chopped, optional
1 onion, chopped
1 teaspoon black pepper
1 cup cracker crumbs
Paprika

Spray Pam on a 9 x 13 inch glass baking dish. Place cauliflower in dish; cover with plastic wrap, leaving one corner open. Cook on high in the microwave for 3 minutes. Turn pan and cook another 3 minutes on high. In a medium saucepan, combine egg, mayonnaise, chicken soup and grated cheese. Heat just until well mixed. Add celery, bell pepper, onion and black pepper to the cauliflower and mix well. Pour soup mixture over vegetables; spread out. Sprinkle cracker crumbs on top. Bake in a preheated 350 degree oven for 35 to 40 minutes, Sprinkle paprika over top of casserole before serving.

Fiesta Corn

1 (16 ounce) can cream style corn
1 (16 ounce) can whole kernel corn, drained
1 bell pepper, chopped
1 small onion, chopped
1 (4 ounce) can chopped green chilies
¼ stick margarine, melted
2 eggs
1 tablespoon sugar
½ teaspoon salt
½ teaspoon pepper
½ cup buttery cracker crumbs
2 tablespoons grated parmesan cheese
1 cup grated Cheddar cheese

Topping:

¾ buttery cracker crumbs
2 tablespoons grated parmesan cheese
Paprika to garnish

Grease a 9 x 13 inch baking dish. In a large mixing bowl, mix together all ingredients except topping and pour into the baking dish. Top with cracker crumbs and parmesan and garnish with the paprika. Bake in a 350 degree oven for 45 minutes. Serves 8 to 10.

Shoe Peg Corn

EASY

1 stick margarine
1 (8 ounce) package cream cheese
3 (16 ounce) cans shoe peg corn, drained
1 (4 ounce) can chopped green chilies
½ teaspoon seasoned salt
½ teaspoon white pepper
1½ cups crushed cracker crumbs

Melt margarine in a large saucepan and stir in cream cheese. Mix until well blended. Add corn, chilies, salt and pepper. Mix; pour into a medium baking dish that has been greased. Sprinkle cracker crumbs over casserole. Bake at 350 degrees for 25 minutes. Serves 8 to 10.

A lady from California once called me and said "where can I buy shoe peg corn?" I thought you could buy anything in California, but evidently not where she lived so I boxed up three cans of shoe peg corn and sent it to her. She was very appreciative and loved that corn.

Wild West Corn

1 (8 ounce) package cream cheese
½ cup sour cream
½ cup milk
1 (4 ounce) can chopped green chilies
1 teaspoon salt
1 teaspoon white pepper
1 (2 ounce) jar pimentos, drained
3 (15 ounce) cans whole kernel corn, drained
¼ teaspoon Tabasco
1 cup cracker crumbs

Preheat oven to 350 degrees. In a large saucepan, melt cream cheese, sour cream and milk, stirring constantly. Add green chilies, salt, pepper, pimentos, corn and Tabasco; mix. Pour into a buttered 2 ½ quart baking dish. Bake covered for 25 minutes. Sprinkle cracker crumbs over casserole and cook 10 minutes longer, uncovered. Serves 8 to 10.

Green Chili Hominy

2 (17 ounce) cans hominy, drained
1 (8 ounce) can chopped green chilies
¼ cup finely grated onion
1½ cups grated Cheddar cheese
1 (8 ounce) carton sour cream
¾ teaspoon seasoned salt
¼ teaspoon pepper

Mix all ingredients together and pour into a medium size greased casserole dish. Bake at 350 degrees for 30 to 35 minutes.

Onion Casserole

3 cups cracker crumbs
1 stick margarine, melted, divided
4 cups thinly sliced onions,

Sauce:

1 cup milk
2 eggs, slightly beaten
1 teaspoon seasoned salt
¼ teaspoon pepper
1½ cups grated Cheddar cheese

Combine and mix cracker crumbs and ½ of the margarine. Place in a 9 x 13 inch baking dish. Pat down. Sauté onions in remaining margarine. Spread onions over crust. For sauce, in saucepan, combine milk, eggs, seasoned salt, pepper and cheese. On low heat, cook until cheese melts. Pour sauce over onions. Bake at 300 degrees for 45 minutes or until knife inserted in center of mixture comes out clean. Serve as a replacement for potatoes or rice.

Gingered Peas With Water Chestnuts

2 (10 ounce) packages frozen peas
3 tablespoons margarine
1 (6 ounce) can mushrooms, drained
1 (8 ounce) can water chestnuts, drained
1 bunch green onions, chopped (a few tops)
1 (4 ounce) jar pimento, drained
¾ teaspoon ground ginger
¼ teaspoon nutmeg
1 (14 ounce) can chicken broth
2 tablespoons cornstarch
½ teaspoon salt
¼ teaspoon garlic powder
⅛ teaspoon pepper
3 tablespoon chopped crystallized ginger

In a large saucepan, place the peas, margarine, mushrooms, water chestnuts, green onion, pimento, ginger, nutmeg and all but ¼ cup chicken broth. Cover and simmer over low heat for 6 to 8 minutes. In a cup, blend cornstarch and reserved chicken broth until smooth. Stir into the peas. Cook slowly, stirring constantly, until liquid thickens and boils. Add salt, garlic powder, pepper and crystallized ginger, simmer about 3 minutes longer. Serves 8. This can be done ahead of time and warmed in the oven.

Swiss Cheesy Peas

3 cans baby green peas and onions
1 (8 ounce) carton sour cream
8 ounces Swiss cheese, grated
½ teaspoon pepper
2 cups crushed corn flakes
¼ stick margarine, melted

Drain peas. In a large saucepan, melt sour cream and Swiss cheese, stirring constantly. Add pepper and peas; mix. Pour into a Pam sprayed 3 quart baking dish. Combine crushed corn flakes and margarine and sprinkle over mixture. Bake at 350 degrees for 35 minutes. Serves 10.

Creamed Green Peas

1 (16 ounce) package frozen English peas
¼ stick margarine
1 can cream of celery soup
1 (3 ounce) package cream cheese
1 (8 ounce) can water chestnuts, drained

Place peas in microwave dish and cook in microwave for 8 minutes, turning dish after 4 minutes. In a large saucepan, combine margarine, soup and cream cheese. Cook on medium heat while stirring, until margarine and cream cheese have melted. Add peas and water chestnuts; mix. Serve hot. Serves 8.

Sunshine Green Peas

2 cans LeSueur sweet peas
1 cup sour cream
8 ounces Swiss cheese, grated
½ onion, minced
½ teaspoon pepper
2 cups crushed corn flakes
3 tablespoons margarine

Drain peas well. In a large saucepan, melt the sour cream and Swiss cheese, stirring constantly. Add onion, pepper and peas; mix. Pour into a buttered baking dish. Combine the crushed corn flakes and margarine and sprinkle over peas. Bake at 350 degrees for 30 minutes. Serves 8 to 10.

Black-Eyed Peas and Tomatoes

1 bell pepper, chopped
1 large onion, chopped
2 ribs celery, chopped
¼ stick margarine
2 cans jalapeno black-eyed peas
1 (15 ounce) can stewed tomatoes
1 teaspoon garlic powder
¼ cup catsup
2 teaspoons dry chicken bouillon

Sauté the bell pepper, onion and celery in the margarine (don't overcook, let them stay a little crispy). Add black-eyed peas, stewed tomatoes, garlic powder, catsup and chicken bouillon. Bring to a boil, turn heat down and simmer about 10 minutes. Serves 8.

Spinach Enchiladas

*2 (10 ounce) packages chopped spinach,
thawed and pressed dry*
1 envelope dry onion soup mix
12 ounces shredded Cheddar cheese
12 ounces shredded Monterey Jack cheese (or mozzarella)
12 flour tortillas
2 cups heavy cream

Make sure your spinach has all the water pressed out! In a medium bowl, combine the spinach and onion soup mix. Then blend in one half of the Cheddar cheese and Jack cheeses. Lay out the 12 tortillas and place about 3 heaping tablespoons of the spinach mixture down the middle of a tortilla and roll up the tortillas. Place each filled tortilla, seam side down, into a Pam sprayed 9 x 13 inch baking dish. Pour the cream over enchiladas and sprinkle with remaining cheeses. Bake, covered in a 350 degree oven for 20 minutes. Uncover and bake another 15 minutes longer. Serves 6 to 8.

*This recipe will freeze well. To make ahead of time, freeze
before adding the cream and remaining cheeses.
Thaw in the refrigerator the night before cooking. These
are so good and so much fun to make and serve! Eat them
all because the tortillas get a little tough if reheated.*

Jalapeno Spinach Bake

2 (10 ounce) packages frozen chopped spinach
½ stick margarine
½ cup chopped onion
3 tablespoons flour
⅔ cup milk
½ teaspoon salt
½ teaspoon pepper
½ teaspoon celery salt
½ teaspoon garlic powder
Several dashes of Tabasco
8 ounces jalapeno Velveeta cheese
1 cup cracker crumbs

Cook spinach according to directions. Or the spinach can be microwaved in the box at 5 minutes for each box at high. Just be sure to punch a few holes in tops of boxes. Melt margarine in a large saucepan and add onion and flour; cook a minute or two (don't turn burner so high that the margarine will burn). Add the milk, salt, pepper, celery salt, garlic powder and Tabasco. Cook on low until mixture is thickened. Add Jalapeno cheese that has been cut in chunks and keep on low heat, stirring until cheese has melted. Add spinach to saucepan and stir until blended. Pour into a greased 3 quart baking dish. Top with cracker crumbs. Bake at 350 degrees for 25 minutes. Serves 8 to 10.

Cheesy Spinach

2 (10 ounce) packages frozen, chopped spinach
1 (16 ounce) carton small curd cottage cheese
2½ cups grated sharp Cheddar cheese
4 eggs, beaten
3 tablespoons flour
½ stick margarine, melted
¼ teaspoon garlic salt
½ teaspoon lemon pepper
¼ teaspoon celery salt
1 tablespoon dried onion flakes

Defrost spinach and squeeze out all water. In a large bowl, mix together the spinach, cottage cheese, Cheddar cheese, eggs, flour, margarine, seasonings and onion flakes. Pour into a 2 ½ quart baking dish that has been sprayed with Pam. Bake at 325 degrees for 1 hour. Casserole may be made a day ahead and baked when ready to serve. Serves 8 to 10.

Yummy Yellow Squash

1 cup small curd cottage cheese
1 (3-ounce) package cream cheese, softened
1½ cups Monterey Jack cheese
½ stick margarine, melted
1 (6-ounce) package Stove Top chicken flavor stuffing mix

After squash has been drained well, add pimento, carrot and water chestnuts and mix. In another bowl mix the sour cream, cottage cheese softened cream cheese, Jack cheese and margarine. Mix well with a whisk. Stir in half the stuffing mix and all of the seasoning that comes with the stuffing; fold into the squash. Spoon into a lightly greased 3 quart casserole. Sprinkle remaining stuffing mix over top and bake at 350 degrees for 30 to 35 minutes. Serves 8 to 10.

Baked Squash Olé

4 to 5 cups cooked squash, drained
1 teaspoon salt
½ teaspoon pepper
1 onion, chopped
1 (4 ounce) can chopped green chilies, drained
¾ cup grated Monterey Jack
1 (10¾ ounce) can cream of chicken soup
1 cup sour cream
1 stick margarine, melted
1 package herb dressing mix

Place cooked squash in a mixing bowl and season with salt and pepper; add onion, green chilies, cheese, soup and sour cream. Blend well. Mix margarine and herb dressing mix. Place ½ of the dressing mix in a 9 x 13 inch greased baking dish; pour squash mixture on top. Sprinkle with remaining dressing mix. Bake at 375 degrees for 30 minutes. Serves 10.

Confetti Squash Casserole

1 pound yellow squash, sliced
1 pound zucchini, sliced
1 large onion, finely chopped
1 can cream of chicken soup
1 (8 ounces) carton sour cream
1 (4 ounce) jar chopped pimento, drained
1 (8 ounce) can sliced water chestnuts, drained
2 carrots, grated
1 stick margarine
6 ounces herb stuffing mix

Cook squash, zucchini and onion in salted water for 10 minutes, drain well. Combine the chicken soup, sour cream, pimento, water chestnuts and carrots. Mix well, but gently. Melt margarine in a saucepan and add stuffing mix; mix. Combine stuffing mix and the squash mixture until well blended. Cover and pour into a greased 9 x 13 inch baking dish. In a preheated 350 degree oven, bake for 30 minutes. Serves 8 to 10. This makes a pretty and delicious vegetable dish!

Posh Squash

2 pounds yellow squash, sliced
1 onion, chopped
1½ pound Velveeta cheese, cubed
2 eggs, beaten
1 tablespoon sugar
1 (4 ounce) jar chopped pimento
1 teaspoon salt
1 teaspoon white pepper
6 tablespoons margarine, melted

Topping:
2 cups cracker crumbs
½ stick margarine, melted
1 (6 ounce) can fried onion rings

Boil squash and onion together until tender. Drain and mash with a potato masher. Add cheese; cook, stirring constantly over low heat until cheese is melted. Add remaining ingredients, except topping and blend well. Pour into a 9 x 13 inch greased casserole dish. Mix crumbs and margarine and sprinkle over casserole. Bake at 350 degrees for 45 minutes. Add fried onion rings to top and bake an additional 5 minutes.

Just remember: It could always be worse. — BCJ

Creamy Squash

6 to 8 medium yellow squash
Water
1 (8 ounce) package cream cheese, softened
2 tablespoons margarine
¾ teaspoon salt
¾ teaspoon pepper
½ teaspoon sugar

Cut squash in little pieces and place in a large saucepan. Cover with water and boil 10 to 15 minutes or until tender. Drain liquid off squash and add cream cheese that has been cut in chunks, margarine, salt, pepper and sugar. Cook over low heat, stirring until cream cheese has melted. Serve hot. Serves 8

Zippy Zucchini

4 eggs
2 cups grated Monterey Jack cheese
1 cup grated Cheddar cheese
4 cups grated zucchini
1 (4 ounce) can chopped green chilies
1 (2 ounce) jar sliced pimentos (optional)
1 onion, finely chopped
1 teaspoon Creole seasoning
1 cup crushed croutons
⅓ cup grated Parmesan cheese

Preheat oven to 350 degrees. In a large mixer bowl, beat eggs well. Stir in cheese, zucchini, green chilies, pimentos, onion and Creole seasoning. Mix well. Pour into a well greased 2 quart baking dish. Bake uncovered 35 minutes. Mix together crushed croutons and parmesan cheese. After 35 minutes, sprinkle crouton mixture over casserole and bake another 10 minutes. Serves 8.

Zucchini on the Ritz

3 pounds zucchini, sliced
1 stick margarine
2 tablespoons cornstarch
1 (4-ounce) can evaporated milk
¼ cup milk
½ pound Velveeta cheese, cubed
1 (4 ounce) can chopped green chilies
1 teaspoon seasoned salt
½ teaspoon white pepper
2½ cups crushed Ritz crackers

Boil zucchini until just barely tender (don't overcook). To make white sauce, melt margarine in a large saucepan; add cornstarch, mix; then add milks. Cook on low heat until white sauce is thick, stir in cheese and heat just until cheese is melted. Add chilies, salt and pepper and fold in cooked, well-drained zucchini. Pour into a greased 9 x13 baking dish and top with cracker crumbs. Bake at 325 degrees for 30 to 35 minutes or until hot and bubbly. To make the day before, leave off cracker crumbs until just before cooking. Serves 8 to 10.

Vegetable Frittata

3 tablespoons oil
1 onion, chopped
¾ cup chopped green bell pepper
¾ cup chopped red bell pepper
2 cups chopped zucchini
2 cups chopped yellow squash
¼ cup half and half
1 (8 ounce) package cream cheese, cubed
6 eggs
1 cup shredded Mozarella cheese
¾ teaspoon garlic powder
1 teaspoon salt
½ teaspoon black pepper
2 teaspoons white wine Worcestershire sauce
1 cup breadcrumbs
2 tablespoons margarine, melted

Heat oil in large skillet. Sauté onion, bell peppers, zucchini and yellow squash (cook just under tender crisp). Remove from heat and set aside to cool. In mixer bowl, beat half and half and the cream cheese until creamy. Add the eggs and beat about 4 minutes until both are well mixed. Mixing by hand, add the cheeses, garlic, salt, black pepper and Worcestershire. Mix breadcrumbs and melted margarine; then add to the cheese mixture. Fold in the vegetables. Pour into a greased 9 inch springform pan. Bake at 350 degrees for 55 to 60 minutes or until lightly browned and set in center. Set out of oven for 10 minutes before slicing to serve. (Be sure to use a knife to cut around the edge of the springform pan before you open the pan).

This makes an elegant dish; perfect for a brunch or late supper.

Spicy Vegetable Couscous

1 (5.7 ounce) package herbed chicken couscous
2 tablespoons margarine
3 tablespoons oil
1 small yellow squash, diced
1 small zucchini, diced
½ red onion, diced
1 red bell pepper, diced
1 (10 ounce) package frozen green peas, thawed
½ teaspoon garlic powder
½ teaspoon ground cumin
½ teaspoon curry powder
½ teaspoon red or cayenne pepper
½ teaspoon salt
½ teaspoon seasoned salt
1 cup shredded Mozzarella cheese

Cook couscous according to package directions, adding 3 tablespoons margarine instead of amount called for. In a large skillet, heat oil and sauté squash, zucchini, onion and bell pepper for about 10 minutes: do not brown. Add peas, garlic powder, cumin, curry powder, red bell pepper, salt and seasoned salt and toss. Combine vegetables and couscous; if it seems a little dry, add a few tablespoons of water. Pour into a Pam sprayed 2 quart or 9 x 13 inch baking dish and sprinkle with Mozzarella cheese. This may be refrigerated and heated later. Set out of refrigerator for an hour or so, then heat at 350 degrees for about 20 minutes. If you don't like it HOT, HOT use only ¼ teaspoon red pepper. Serves 10 to 12.

This is not only really good, it is a colorful dish!

The Ultimate Potato

6 large baking potatoes, boiled
¾ stick margarine, melted
½ pound Cheddar cheese, grated
1 cup sour cream
½ cup chopped green onions
6 strips bacon, fried and crumbled

Peel cooled potatoes and grate. Combine cream, margarine, cheese and sour cream in double boiler and stir just until melted. Add cheese mixture to grated potatoes and put in a greased casserole dish. Bake at 350 degrees for 30 minutes. Top with onions and bacon. Bake another 5 minutes. Serves 8.

Don't count the calories here!

Creamy Mashed Potatoes

6 large potatoes
1 (8 ounce) carton sour cream
1 (8 ounce) package cream cheese, softened
1 teaspoon salt
½ teaspoon white pepper

This can be made the day before and reheated. Peel, cut up and boil the potatoes. Drain. Whip until cream cheese has melted. Pour into greased 3 quart baking dish. Cover with foil and bake at 325 degrees for about 20 minutes. (About 10 minutes longer if you are reheating them.) Serves 8 to 10.

Scalloped Potatoes

6 medium potatoes
1 stick margarine
Black pepper
1 tablespoon flour
2 cups grated Cheddar cheese
¾ cup milk

Preheat oven to 350 degrees. Peel and wash potatoes. Slice ½ of the potatoes and place in a 3 quart greased baking dish. Slice the stick of margarine and place ½ over potatoes. Sprinkle with pepper. Sprinkle flour over top of pepper. Cover with half the cheese. Slice remaining potatoes; place over first layers; add remaining margarine slices. Pour milk over casserole and sprinkle a little more pepper. Cover with remaining cheese. Cover and bake for 1 hour. This must be cooked immediately or potatoes will darken; it can be frozen after baking and then reheated. Serves 8.

New Potatoes and Herb Butter

1½ pounds new potatoes
¼ stick butter, sliced
¼ teaspoon thyme
½ cup chopped fresh parsley
½ teaspoon rosemary

Scrub potatoes and cut in halves; do not peel. In medium saucepan, boil in lightly salted water. Cook until potatoes are tender, about 15 minutes. Drain. Add butter, thyme, parsley and rosemary. Toss gently until butter is melted. Serves 8.

Sweet Potato Casserole

1 (29 ounce) can sweet potatoes, drained
⅓ cup evaporated milk
¾ cup sugar
2 eggs, beaten
½ stick margarine, melted
1 teaspoon vanilla

Topping:
1 cup packed light brown sugar
⅓ cup margarine, melted
½ cup flour
1 cup chopped pecans

Heat oven to 350 degrees. Place sweet potatoes in a mixing bowl and mash slightly with fork. Add evaporated milk, sugar, eggs, margarine and vanilla. Mix well. Pour into a greased 7 x 11 inch baking dish. Mix topping ingredients together and sprinkle over top of casserole. Bake, uncovered, for 35 minutes or until crusty on top. Serves 8.

This has become a Thanksgiving regular for us.
Even sweet potato haters like this a lot.

Cheddar Potato Casserole

1 (2 pound) bag frozen hash brown potatoes, thawed
1 onion, finely chopped
1 stick margarine, melted
1 cup sour cream
1 can cream of chicken soup
2 cups grated Cheddar cheese
1½ cups corn flakes, crushed
½ stick margarine, melted

In a large mixing bowl, combine hash browns, onion, margarine, sour cream, soup and cheese; mix well. Pour into a greased 9 x 13 inch baking dish. Combine corn flakes and melted margarine and sprinkle on casserole. Bake
at 350 degrees for 45 minutes.

This is a "winner" for the easiest and best potato dish!

Spanish Sunset Rice

½ cup rice, uncooked
1 onion, chopped
¾ stick margarine, melted
½ cup chopped bell pepper
¾ cup water
1 (16-ounce) can stewed tomatoes
1 teaspoon salt
¼ teaspoon paprika
½ teaspoon seasoned pepper
1 cup grated Cheddar cheese

Mix all ingredients together and pour into a greased 9 x 13 inch Pyrex baking dish and cook covered with foil at 350 degrees for about 50 minutes. Serves 8.

Three Cheese Manicotti

1½ cups water
1 (8 ounce) can tomato sauce
1 (1½ ounce) package spaghetti sauce mix
2½ cups grated mozzarella cheese, divided
1 cup ricotta or small curd cottage cheese
½ cup grated Parmesan cheese
2 eggs, beaten
½ teaspoon salt
¼ teaspoon pepper
8 manicotti shells

Combine water, tomato sauce and spaghetti sauce mix in a small saucepan. Simmer, uncovered about 10 minutes. In mixing bowl, combine 1 cup mozzarella cheese, ricotta, Parmesan, eggs, salt and pepper; stir gently and set aside. Cook manicotti shells according to package directions; drain. Stuff cheese mixture into manicotti shells, using about ¼ cup for each shell. Pour ½ cup sauce into a 9 x 13 inch baking pan; arrange manicotti shells in sauce. Pour remaining sauce over top. Sprinkle with remaining Mozzarella cheese. Bake, uncovered at 350 degrees for 30 minutes or until bubbly. Serves 4.

Make the best of a bad situation. — BCJ

Carnival Couscous

1 (5.7 ounce) package Herbed Chicken Flavor Couscous
1¼ cups water
2 tablespoons margarine
Spice Sack (in the couscous)
1 tablespoons margarine
1 cup chopped red bell pepper
1 cup chopped green bell pepper
¾ cup coarsely shredded carrots
1 bunch green onion, chopped (some tops too)
8 small fresh mushrooms, thinly sliced (optional)
½ teaspoon garlic powder
1 teaspoon dried dill weed
½ teaspoon salt
½ teaspoon seasoned salt
½ teaspoon black pepper

In a large saucepan, cook the couscous with the water, margarine and Spice Sack as directed on the package. In a skillet, place the 3 tablespoons margarine, both bell peppers, carrots, onions and mushrooms; cook on medium heat about 8 to 10 minutes. Add the garlic, dill weed, salt, seasoned salt and black pepper. Spoon the pepper-carrot mixture into the couscous (if the couscous seem a little too dry, add a tablespoon or two of water). Serve immediately or place in casserole and warm in a 300 degree oven for about 20 minutes. This is really better made the same day and not having been refrigerated then warmed up. Serves 6 to 8.

*This side dish is a rainbow of colors- delightful
looking as well as delicious!*

Cornbread Dress.

2 packages cornbread mix, pre,
9 biscuits or 1 recipe of Bisquick biscui.
1 small onion, choppe.
2 celery stalks, chopped
2 eggs
Black pepper
2 teaspoons poultry seasoning
3 (14 ½ ounce) cans chicken broth

Gravy:

2 cans chicken broth
2 heaping tablespoons cornstarch
Black pepper
2 boiled eggs, sliced (optional)

Prepare cornbread and biscuits ahead. Crumble cornbread and biscuits into a large bowl using a little more cornbread than biscuits. Add onion, celery, eggs and seasonings. Stir in 2 ½ cans of the broth. If the mixture is not "runny", add the rest of the broth. (If it is still not runny, add a little milk.) Bake in a Pam sprayed 9 x 13 inch glass baking dish at 350 degrees for about 45 minutes or until golden brown. This can be frozen uncooked; just thaw before cooking.

FOR THE GRAVY: In a saucepan, mix the cornstarch with a half cup of the broth — mixed with no lumps. Then add the remaining broth and heat to boiling, stirring constantly until broth thickens. Add boiled eggs.

Jazzy Turkey and Dressing

1 (8 ounce) package stuffing
3 cups diced, cooked turkey
1 (15 ounce) can golden hominy, drained
1 (4 ounce) can chopped green chilies, drained
½ cup chopped red bell pepper
2 tablespoons dried parsley flakes
1 can cream of chicken soup, undiluted
1 (8 ounce) carton sour cream
½ cup water
¼ stick margarine, melted
2 teaspoons ground cumin
½ teaspoon salt
1 cup shredded mozzarella cheese

In a large mixing bowl, combine all ingredients except cheese. Mix well and pour into a greased 9 x 13 inch baking dish; cover with foil. Bake at 350 degrees for 35 minutes. Uncover; sprinkle with cheese and bake an additional 5 minutes. Serves 10 to 12.

Mind your manners.

Orange Spiced Chicken

6 large chicken breast halves, boned, skinned
2/3 cup flour
1 teaspoon salt
½ teaspoon white pepper
¼ teaspoon dried basil
¼ teaspoon dried oregano
¼ teaspoon dried marjoram
¼ teaspoon leaf tarragon
2 or 3 tablespoons oil
1 (6 ounce) can frozen orange juice concentrate, thawed
¼ cup water
½ cup white wine vinegar
2/3 cup packed brown sugar

Mix flour, salt, pepper and spices together in a baggie. Pour oil into a large skillet and heat. Coat chicken in flour mixture, one or two pieces of chicken at a time. Brown both sides of the chicken breasts. In a small bowl, mix the orange juice, water, vinegar and brown sugar. When the chicken breasts are browned, place them in a large Pam sprayed baking dish. Cover with the orange juice mixture and bake, uncovered in a 325 degree oven for one hour. Serve over rice.

For a lovely presentation of this dish, I like to use a 6.2 ounce box of Uncle Ben's long grain and wild rice. After the chicken has cooked, it can stand out of the oven for an hour or so; then before you want to serve the chicken, cook the rice, as directed on box and place in a 9 x 13 inch Pyrex dish. Then spoon each chicken breasts on top of the rice and pour the remaining orange juice sauce over the top. About 15 minutes in a 325 degree oven will warm it to just the right temperature for serving. A"10" all the way!

Saucy Chicken Breasts

1½ cups mayonnaise
½ cup cider vinegar
¼ cup lemon juice
3 tablespoons sugar
3 tablespoons white Wine Worcestershire
(It must be the WHITE Worcestershire.)
6 chicken breasts, thawed, skinned
Seasoned pepper

In a saucepan, combine mayonnaise, vinegar, lemon juice, sugar and Worcestershire and mix well with a wire whisk until mixture is smooth. Pour HALF into a baggie with the chicken breasts and marinate for 4 to 6 hours. Move chicken around a couple of times to make sure marinade is on the chicken. Preheat oven to 350 degrees. When ready to cook, place chicken breasts in a large pan (so that each breast is separate and not touching) and pour marinade from baggie over chicken. Sprinkle pepper GENEROUSLY over breasts. Cook uncovered for 50 to 60 minutes. If the chicken breasts have not browned slightly, place under broiler for 3 to 4 minutes (watch closely). However, if your oven heats pretty hot, don't let the sauce that is between the chicken breasts get brown. It will be done when the sauce is just LIGHTLY brown. Heat remaining half of the sauce, adding several dashes of the seasoned pepper, to serve a spoonful over the chicken. This sauce really makes a delicious chicken dish!

Your mother will always
be your mother. — BCJ

191

Poppy Seed Chicken

8 chicken breasts, boned, skinned
1 can cream of chicken soup
1 (8 ounce) carton sour cream
½ cup dry white wine (or cooking wine)
1½ cups Ritz cracker crumbs (1 stack)
1 cup almonds, toasted and chopped
1 stick margarine, melted
Poppy seeds

Place chicken breasts in a buttered 9 x 13 inch baking pan. Set aside. In a saucepan, combine soup, sour cream and wine; heat just until it has been mixed. Pour soup mixture over chicken. Combine cracker crumbs, almonds and margarine. Sprinkle over casserole. Sprinkle with poppy seeds and bake at 350 degrees for 45 minutes. This can be served over rice or noodles.

Apricot Chicken

1 cup apricot preserves
1 (8 ounce) bottle Catalina dressing
1 package onion soup mix
8 chicken breasts

In a bowl, mix apricot preserves, dressing and soup mix. Place chicken breasts in a large, buttered baking dish and pour apricot mixture over chicken. Bake uncovered at 325 degrees for I hour and 20 minutes. Serve over hot rice.

When you're in a rush, this is the recipe! And it is super good! Try it with one of the spinach salads on pages 125 or 128 and the green bean recipes on pages 151-152. For really fast meals, get the ready-made salad from the grocery store and you're still a genius.

Hawaiian Chicken

2 medium-sized chickens, cut in quarters (skin removed)
Salt and pepper for chicken
Flour to coat chicken
Oil
1 can (20-ounce) can sliced pineapple
1 cup sugar
3 tablespoons cornstarch
¾ cup vinegar
1 tablespoon soy sauce
¼ teaspoon ginger
2 chicken bouillon cubes
1 tablespoon lemon juice
2 bell peppers, cut in strips
Cooked rice

Wash chicken and pat dry with paper towel. Coat chicken with salt, pepper and flour. Brown chicken quarters in oil and place in large shallow roasting pan. To make sauce, drain pineapple, pouring syrup into a 2 cup measure. Add water (or orange juice) to make 1½ cups. In medium saucepan, combine sugar, cornstarch, pineapple syrup, vinegar, soy sauce, ginger, bouillon cubes and lemon juice and bring to a boil. Stir constantly for about 2 minutes - until thickened and dear. Pour over browned chicken. Bake at 350 degrees, covered for 40 minutes. Place pineapple slices and bell pepper on top of chicken and bake 10 to 15 minutes longer. Serve on fluffy white rice. Serves 8.

This is an old recipe that is a family favorite from years ago when we had to cut up our own chicken.

Succulent Pecan Chicken Breasts

⅓ cup margarine
1 cup flour
1 cup pecans, finely ground
¼ cup sesame seeds
1 tablespoon paprika
1teaspoon salt
¼ teaspoon pepper
1 egg, beaten
1 cup buttermilk
6 large or 8 small chicken breasts, skinned and boned
⅓ cup coarsely chopped pecans

Melt margarine in a large 9 x 13 inch baking dish. set aside. Combine flour, finely ground pecans, sesame seeds, paprika, salt and pepper. Combine egg and buttermilk in a separate bowl. Dip chicken in egg mixture and dredge in flour mixture, coating well. Place chicken in baking dish turning once to coat with the margarine. Sprinkle with chopped pecans. Bake in a 350 degree preheated oven for about 40 to 45 minutes. Chicken should be golden brown. Garnish with fresh parsley or sage.

Chicken can be cut into strips and prepared the same way to be used as an appetizer. A honey mustard dressing would be nice for dipping.

You could use this same recipe for fish, like an orange roughy, but reduce cooking time by half

Cilantro Chicken Cutlets

1 teaspoon seasoned salt

1 teaspoon seasoned pepper

2 teaspoons cilantro

1 teaspoon cumin

6 boned chicken breasts, pounded into ¼ inch thick pieces

2 cups breadcrumbs

Oil

3 tablespoons margarine

¼ cup flour

½ teaspoon salt

1 teaspoon seasoned pepper

¼ teaspoon cumin

1 teaspoon cilantro

2 cups milk

⅓ cup dry white wine

1 cup grated Monterey Jack cheese

Mix together seasoned salt, seasoned pepper, cilantro, and cumin. Sprinkle seasonings over chicken cutlets and dip in breadcrumbs. Pour oil into a large skillet and brown chicken. Remove to a 9 x 13 inch greased baking dish. In a saucepan, melt margarine, blend in flour and seasonings. Add milk and stirring constantly, cook until thickened. Remove from heat and stir in wine. Pour sauce over chicken and bake at 350 degrees for 45 minutes. Remove from oven and sprinkle cheese on top of each piece of chicken; return to oven for 5 minutes. Serves 6.

Sesame Chicken

½ cup flour
½ teaspoon chili powder
¼ teaspoon paprika
½ teaspoon onion salt
½ teaspoon celery salt
1 teaspoon lemon pepper
1 teaspoon garlic powder
8 skinned chicken breasts
1 stick margarine, melted
1 cup sesame seeds, lightly toasted

Thoroughly mix flour, chili powder, paprika, onion and celery salt, lemon pepper and garlic powder. Roll chicken breasts in flour mixture; keep rolling chicken until all flour mixture is used up. Dip floured chicken in margarine and then roll in sesame seeds. Place chicken breasts into a greased 9 x 13 baking dish. Pour any extra margarine in baking dish. Bake at 325 degrees for 1 hour.

Three Cheers for Chicken

8 chicken breasts, boned and skinned
Salt and pepper
¾ stick margarine
1 onion, chopped
½ bell pepper, chopped
1 small jar chopped pimentos
1 cup uncooked rice
1 can cream of chicken soup
1 can cream of celery soup
2 cans water
1 can sliced water chestnuts
1 cup grated Cheddar cheese

Salt and pepper chicken and place in a large 11 x 14 inch pyrex. Melt margarine and add onion, bell pepper, pimentos, rice, soups, water and water chestnuts and pour over chicken breasts. Cook at 350 degrees for 15 minutes, then turn oven down to 325 degrees and cook for 1 hour more. Add cheese 5 minutes before dish is done and return to oven for the last 5 minutes.

So easy to put together and so good an hour and 15 minutes later!

Oven Herb Chicken

2 cups crushed corn flakes
½ cup grated Parmesan cheese
1 tablespoon rosemary
1 tablespoon thyme leaves
1 teaspoon oregano
1 tablespoon parsley flakes
½ teaspoon garlic powder
½ teaspoon salt
1 teaspoon black pepper
8 chicken breasts, skinned, boned or 1 chicken, quartered
1 stick margarine, melted

In a medium bowl, mix cornflakes, Parmesan cheese, rosemary, thyme, oregano, parsley, garlic powder, salt and pepper. Melt margarine in a small bowl in the microwave and dip chicken breasts in melted margarine and then in the cornflakes mixture, coating well. Place in a shallow greased 9 x 13 inch baking dish. Do not crowd pieces. Bake, uncovered at 325 degrees for 1 hour.

I started using this recipe when "they" started telling us we shouldn't eat "fried chicken"! My husband decided he could live without "fried chicken" if I "fried" the chicken this way.

Sweet and Sour Chicken

8 chicken breasts, skinned and boned
Oil
1 package onion soup mix
1 (6 ounce) can frozen orange juice concentrate, thawed
2/3 cup water

In a skillet, brown chicken breasts in a little oil. Place chicken breasts in a greased 9 x 13 inch glass baking dish. In a small bowl, combine onion soup mix, orange juice and water. Stir well, making sure the lumps of seasoning in the onion soup mix are diluted. Pour over chicken breasts. Bake uncovered at 350 degrees for 45 minutes.

South of the Border Chicken

8 chicken breasts, boned and skinned
1 cup grated Monterey Jack cheese
½ cup Cheddar cheese
1 (4 ounce) can chopped green chilies
1 teaspoon cilantro
3 tablespoons dehydrated onion
⅓ cup margarine
2 teaspoons cumin
1 teaspoon chili powder
Tortilla chips, crushed

Pound chicken breasts flat. In bowl, mix cheeses, chilies, cilantro and onion. Place 2 to 3 tablespoons of cheese mixture on each chicken breast and roll up, placing seam side down in a greased casserole dish. In a saucepan, melt margarine; add cumin and chili powder. Pour over chicken. Bake covered for 45 minutes at 350 degrees. Uncover and top with crushed chips. Return to oven and bake 3 more minutes.

Chicken Fiesta

1 stick margarine
2 cups finely crushed cheese crackers
2 tablespoons taco seasoning mix
8 chicken breasts, boned, skinned and flattened
1 bunch green onions, chopped, tops too
1 teaspoon dry chicken bouillon
2 cups heavy cream
2 cups grated Monterey Jack cheese
1 (4 ounce) can chopped green chilies

Melt margarine in a 9 x 13 inch baking dish and set aside. Combine cracker crumbs and taco mix. Dredge chicken in this mixture, patting the mixture in so you get plenty of crumbs to stick to the chicken. Place chicken breasts in baking dish with margarine. In a saucepan, take out a couple tablespoons of the melted margarine and place in a saucepan. Add onions and sauté. Turn heat off and add chicken bouillon; stir. Add heavy cream, Monterey Jack cheese, and chopped green chilies; mix well. Pour over chicken in baking dish. Bake uncovered at 350 degrees for 55 minutes.

Life is not a matter of milestones,
but of moments.
— Rose Kennedy

Lemon Herb Chicken

1 stick margarine
8 chicken breasts, skinned
1 cup flour

Lemon Herb sauce:
¼ cup lemon juice
½ teaspoon salt
½ teaspoon lemon pepper
½ teaspoon garlic powder
2 tablespoons brown sugar
½ teaspoon oregano
½ teaspoon crushed rosemary
1 teaspoon lemon peel
½ cup hot water
Hot cooked rice
Lemon slices, optional

Preheat oven to 350 degrees. Melt the margarine in the microwave in a medium size mixing bowl. Spoon off about 2 tablespoons and place in 9 x 13 inch baking dish; smooth across pan. Dip each chicken breast in margarine and then in flour. Place the floured chicken in the baking dish. Cover with foil and bake 30 minutes. While chicken is cooking, add all ingredients of the Lemon Herb sauce to the mixing bowl with the remaining margarine; mix well. After chicken has cooked the 30 minutes, remove foil covering and pour Lemon Herb sauce over chicken. Bake another 25 minutes. Serve over cooked white rice. Use lemon slices for garnish.

Chicken and Tortilla Dumplings

6 large chicken breasts, skinned and boned
9 to 10 cups water to cover chicken
2 celery ribs, chopped
1 small onion, chopped
About 2 tablespoons of chicken bouillon
1 can cream of chicken soup undiluted
10 or 11 (8 inch) flour tortillas

In a large kettle or roaster, place the chicken breasts, water, celery and onion. Bring to a boil, then reduce heat and cook for about 30 minutes – until chicken is tender. Remove chicken, reserving broth in the roaster (you should have about 8 to 9 cups of broth) . Let chicken cool and cut into bite size pieces. Gradually add some of the bouillon. I suggest you taste to make sure the broth is rich and tasty. Add the chicken soup and bring to a boil Cut tortillas into 2 x 1 inch strips. Add strips, one at a time, to briskly boiling broth mixture while stirring constantly. Add chicken, reduce heat and simmer 5 to 10 minutes, stirring often to prevent dumplings from sticking. Serves 8.

Flour tortillas make wonderful dumplings. You can't tell them from the real thing. And they are so good! Easy too!

Jalapeno Chicken

2 cups chopped onion
2 tablespoons margarine
1 (10 ounce) package frozen spinach, cooked and drained
6 jalapenos or 1 (7 ounce) can green chilies
1 (8 ounce) carton sour cream
2 cans cream of chicken soup
4 green onion tops, chopped
½ teaspoon salt
1 (12 ounce) package Doritos, slightly crushed
4 cups diced turkey (or chicken)
1 (8 ounce) package shredded Monterey Jack cheese

Sauté onion in margarine. Blend in spinach, peppers, sour cream, soups, onion tops and salt. In a large 15x10 inch baking dish (or two 9 x 9 inch), alternate Doritos, chicken, spinach mixture and cheese. Repeat layers with the cheese on top. Bake 35 minutes at 350 degrees.

Even if you are not a spinach fan, you will find this to your liking!

203

...n and Ham Tetrazzini

...ounce) package spaghetti, cooked and drained
½ cup slivered almonds, toasted
1 can cream of mushroom soup
1 can cream of chicken soup
¾ cup milk
2 tablespoons dry white wine
2½ cups diced chicken
2 cups fully cooked, diced ham
½ cup chopped green bell pepper
½ cup halved pitted ripe olives
1 (8 ounce) package shredded Cheddar cheese

Rinse cooked spaghetti with cold water to maintain firmness. Mix together almonds, soups, milk and wine in dish. Stir in spaghetti, chicken, ham, chopped pepper and pitted olives. Pour into a Pam sprayed 9 x 13 inch baking dish. Sprinkle top of mixture with the Cheddar cheese. Bake uncovered for 35 minutes at 350 degrees or until hot and bubbly. Serves 10.

Creamy Turkey Enchiladas

2 tablespoons margarine
1 onion, finely chopped
3 green onions, chopped, tops too
½ teaspoon garlic powder
½ teaspoon seasoned salt
1 (7 ounce) can chopped green chilies
2 (8 ounce) packages of cream cheese, softened
3 cups diced turkey or chicken
8 (8 inch) flour tortillas
2 (8 ounce) cartons whipping cream
1 (16 ounce) package shredded Monterey Jack cheese

In a large skillet, add margarine and sauté onions. Add garlic powder, seasoned salt and green chilies. Stir in cream cheese. Heat and stir until cream cheese is melted. Add diced chicken. Lay out the 8 tortillas and spoon about 3 heaping tablespoons of the turkey mixture on each tortilla. Roll up tortillas and place seam side down in a lightly greased large 9 ½ x 13 ½ inch baking dish. Pour whipping cream over enchiladas; then sprinkle the cheese over the enchiladas. Bake uncovered at 350 degrees for 35 minutes.

Forget about the calories. These enchiladas are worth it.
They are one of my favorites.

Divine Chicken Casserole

1 (16 ounce) package frozen broccoli spears
1 teaspoon seasoned salt
3 cups diced, cooked chicken
1 can cream of chicken soup (undiluted)
2 tablespoons milk
1/3 cup mayonnaise
2 teaspoons lemon juice
1/4 teaspoon black pepper
3 tablespoons melted margarine
1 cup bread crumbs (or cracker crumbs)
1/3 cup shredded Cheddar cheese

Cook broccoli as directed on package; drain. Place broccoli in a 8 x 12 inch Pam sprayed glass baking dish and sprinkle seasoned salt over the broccoli. Cover with the diced chicken. In a saucepan, combine soup, milk, mayonnaise, lemon juice and pepper. Heat just enough to dilute the soup a little; pour over the chicken. Mix melted margarine, breadcrumbs and cheese and sprinkle over soup mixture. Bake uncovered in a preheated 350 degree oven for 30 minutes or until mixture is hot and bubbly. Serves 6.

Chinese Chicken

3½ cups cooked chicken, cut in bite size chunks
2 cans cream of chicken soup
1 (16 ounce) can Chop Suey vegetables, drained
1 (8 ounce) can sliced water chestnuts, drained
¾ cup cashew nuts
1 cup chopped green peppers
1 bunch green onions, sliced, tops too
½ cup chopped celery
⅓ teaspoon Tabasco
¼ teaspoon curry powder
1 (5 ounce) can Chow Mein noodles

In a large bowl, combine chicken, soups, vegetables, water chestnuts, cashew nuts, green pepper, green onions, celery, Tabasco and curry powder. Stir to mix well. Spoon into a Pam sprayed 9 x 13 inch glass baking dish. Sprinkle Chow Mein noodles over top of casserole. Bake uncovered at 350 degrees for 30 to 35 minutes or until bubbly at edges of casserole. Let set 5 minutes before serving. Serves 10.

Three Cheese Chicken Casserole

1 (8 ounce) package egg noodles
3 quarts water
1 tablespoon salt
1 teaspoon oil
3 tablespoons margarine
¾ cup chopped green bell pepper
½ cup chopped celery
½ cup chopped onion
1 can cream of chicken soup
½ cup milk
1 (6 ounce) jar whole mushrooms
½ teaspoon black pepper
1 (12 ounce) carton small-curd cottage cheese
4 cups diced turkey (or chicken)
1 (12 ounce) package shredded Cheddar cheese
¾ cup freshly grated Parmesan

In a large kettle, place noodles in hot water; add salt and oil. Cook according to package instructions. Melt margarine in a skillet and sauté the bell pepper, celery and onion. In a large bowl, combine noodles, sautéed mixture, chicken soup, milk, mushrooms, black pepper, cottage cheese, chicken and Cheddar cheese. Pour into a Pam sprayed 9 x 13 inch baking dish. Top with the Parmesan cheese. Bake uncovered at 350 degrees for 40 minutes. Serves 10.

Dorito Delight

3½ cups cooked, diced turkey (or chicken)
1 (16 ounce) bag Doritos
1 onion, chopped
3 stalks celery, chopped
1 can cream of chicken soup
2 (10 ounce) cans tomatoes and green chilies
1 pound Velveeta cheese, cut in chunks

Pam spray a 9 x 13 inch baking dish and place ½ of the bag of Doritos in dish. Crush a little with the palm of your hand. In a large saucepan, combine onion, celery, chicken soup, tomatoes and green chilies and Velveeta. On medium heat, stir until cheese is melted. Add chicken pieces and pour over Doritos. Crush remaining Doritos in a baggie with a rolling pin. Sprinkle over chicken-cheese mixture. Bake at 350 degrees about 35 minutes or until bubbly around edges. Serves 8 to 10.

Busy Day Chicken Casserole

6 chicken breasts, cooked and sliced in strips
2 (8 ounce) cartons sour cream
1 (7 ounce) package ready-cut spaghetti - NOT COOKED
2 cans cream of chicken soup
1 (4 ounce) can mushrooms, drained
1 stick margarine, melted
⅛ teaspoon pepper
1 cup fresh grated Parmesan cheese

Combine all ingredients except the Parmesan cheese. Pour into a greased 9 x 13 inch casserole dish. Sprinkle cheese on top. Bake, covered in a preheated 350 degree oven for 50 minutes.
*So **Easy** and So Good!*

Taco Casserole

1 can cream of mushroom soup
1 can cream of chicken soup
1 cup milk
1 envelope taco seasoning
1 onion, chopped
½ teaspoon celery salt
1 (4 ounce) can chopped green chilies
5 to 6 chicken breasts, cooked
1 package corn tortillas or Doritos
2 cups grated Cheddar cheese
2 cups Monterey Jack cheese

Combine soups, milk, taco seasoning, onion, celery salt and green chilies. Cut chicken breasts into bite-size pieces. Combine grated cheeses. In a 9 x 13 inch pyrex, layer the following twice: Doritos, chicken, soup mixture and cheese. Cheese will be on top. Bake uncovered at 325 degrees for 1 hour.

Old Fashioned Chicken Spaghetti

8 to 10 ounces spaghetti
1 bell pepper, chopped
1 onion, chopped
1 cup chopped celery
1 stick margarine
1 can tomato soup
1 can Rotel diced tomatoes and green chilies
1 small can chopped mushrooms
½ teaspoon salt
½ teaspoon pepper
½ teaspoon garlic powder
3 teaspoons chicken bouillon
½ cup water
4 to 5 cups chopped chicken or turkey
8 ounces Velveeta cheese, chopped
8 ounces Cheddar cheese, chopped

Cook spaghetti according to package instructions. Drain. In a medium saucepan, sauté bell pepper, onion and celery in margarine. Add soup, Rotel tomatoes, mushrooms, salt, pepper, garlic powder, bouillon and water, mix. In a large mixing bowl, mix spaghetti, soup and tomato mixture, chicken and cheese. Place in 2 greased, 2-quart casseroles. Freeze one and bake the other (covered) for 40 to 50 minutes at 325 degrees. To cook the frozen casserole, thaw first. This is a good recipe to use leftover turkey.

Chicken Ole'

Oil
3 onions, chopped
3 bell peppers, chopped
1 teaspoon garlic powder
2 cans Rotel tomatoes and chilies
1 pound Velveeta cheese, cut in chunks
1 pound Cheddar cheese, grated
6 cups cooked, chopped chicken
1 pint sour cream
1 (3-ounce) jar pimentos
Cooked rice
Small Fritos

Cook the onion, bell pepper and garlic in a little bit of oil. Add the tomatoes and green chilies and bring to a boil. Reduce heat and simmer until thick, about 15 minutes. Add the cheeses and heat slowly until cheese is melted. Add chicken, sour cream and pimentos. Heat until hot but do not boil. Serve over a layer of rice and a layer of small Fritos. Serves 12.

When eating this delicious chicken, you get a surprise "crunch" because when you pour the chicken mixture over the rice and Fritos, you don't see the Fritos – "surprise crunch"!

Chicken and Sausage Extraordinaire

1 (6 ounce) box Uncle Ben's Long Grain and Wild Rice
1 pound pork sausage
1 pound fresh mushrooms, sliced (optional)
2 onions, chopped
7 large chicken breasts halves, cooked and sliced
3 tablespoons margarine
¼ cup flour
½ cup whipping cream
2½ cups chicken broth
¾ teaspoon seasoned salt
¼ teaspoon pepper
½ stick margarine, melted
2 cups crushed crackers

Cook rice according to directions and set aside. Brown sausage in large skillet. Remove sausage with slotted spoon and sauté mushrooms and onions in sausage fat until onion is transparent. Drain and stir in chicken. set aside. Melt margarine in a saucepan; add flour and mix. Over medium heat, add cream and broth and cook, stirring constantly until mixture resembles a thick white sauce. Pour into a large bowl. Add salt. pepper rice, sausage and chicken mixture. Mix thoroughly. Place in a Pam sprayed 9 x 13 inch baking dish. Mix together be melted margarine and crushed crackers; sprinkle over casserole. Bake in a preheated 350 degree oven for 25 to 30 minutes. Serves 10 to 12. This can be frozen; thaw in refrigerator and make sure it is thawed in the middle before reheating.

Chicken Broccoli Casserole

8 chicken breasts, cooked and sliced
1 stick margarine
½ cup flour
2 cups half and half
1 (14½ ounce) can chicken broth
1 (8 ounce) package shredded Cheddar cheese, divided
1 (3 ounce) package fresh Parmesan cheese
2 tablespoons lemon juice
1 tablespoon prepared mustard
¼ teaspoon white pepper
2 tablespoons dried parsley
1 tablespoon dried onion flakes (or 3 tablespoons fresh chopped onion)
2 teaspoons salt
½ teaspoon rosemary
¾ cup mayonnaise
2 (10 ounce) boxes frozen broccoli florets, slightly cooked
1 (7 ounce) package thin spaghetti
Paprika

Prepare chicken. Melt margarine in a VERY large saucepan or roaster. Add flour and mix. Over low to medium heat, gradually add half-and-half, stirring constantly until it has thickened. Add chicken broth, HALF the Cheddar cheese, the Parmesan cheese, lemon juice, white pepper, mustard, parsley, onion, salt and rosemary. Heat on low until cheeses have melted. Remove from heat and add mayonnaise. (To cook the broccoli, you can punch small holes in the broccoli boxes and microwave 4 minutes. You don't want to over-cook the broccoli. Cut off about half of the stems and discard.) Now add the broccoli and the chicken slices to the sauce. Cook the spaghetti by directions on the box. Drain and pour into a 10 x 15 inch pyrex (this will NOT

(Continued on Next Page)

(Continued)

fit in a 9 x 13 inch pyrex). Spread the sauce and chicken mixture over the spaghetti; then sprinkle remaining cheese over the top. Sprinkle a little paprika over top. Cook, uncovered for 40 minutes at 350 degrees.

Chicken Souffle

16 slices white bread, buttered on one side, with crusts removed
6 chicken breast, cooked, boned, skinned and sliced
½ cup mayonnaise
1 cup grated Cheddar cheese, divided
5 large eggs
2 cups milk
1 teaspoon salt
1 can cream of mushroom soup

Butter a 9 x 13 inch baking dish. Line bottom with 8 bread slices. Cover with sliced chicken meat, spread chicken slices with mayonnaise and sprinkle with ½ cup cheese. (You could use deli-sliced chicken instead of cooking the chicken breasts.) Top with remaining 8 slices bread. Beat together eggs milk and salt; pour over entire casserole. Refrigerate overnight or all day. When ready to bake, with the back of a large spoon, spread soup over top. Bake, covered, at 350 degrees for 45 minutes. Uncover, sprinkle with remaining ½ cup Cheddar cheese; return to oven and bake at 350 for 15 minutes longer. Serves 8 to 10.

This is a great luncheon dish. Serve with Broccoli Noodle Crunch page 117 and the Fantastic Fruit Salad on page 98. Flavored ice tea is a nice touch, too.

Finger-Lickin' Smoked Chicken

3 chickens, cut in half
Lawry's seasoned pepper
1 stick margarine
2 teaspoons Worcestershire
2 dashes Tabasco
2 tablespoons lemon juice
½ teaspoon garlic salt
1 can 7-Up

Sprinkle chickens with seasoned pepper and leave at room temperature for 1 hour. Melt margarine with Worcestershire, Tabasco, lemon juice and garlic salt, add 7-Up. Cook chickens on charcoal grill with mesquite charcoal. Turn often and baste with margarine-7-Up mixture several times. When chicken is done (about 60 minutes), baste once more to keep chicken moist.

Yummy Barbecue Grilled Chicken

6 chicken breasts or 1 chicken quartered
3 cups catsup
½ cup packed brown sugar
¼ cup Worcestershire
2 tablespoons vinegar
2 teaspoons seasoned salt
1 teaspoon Tabasco
½ teaspoon cracked black pepper

Dry chicken breasts with paper towels. In a saucepan, combine and mix together the catsup, brown sugar, Worcestershire, vinegar, seasoned salt, Tabasco and pepper. Bring sauce to a boil, reduce heat to low and cook 15 minutes. Fire up the grill,

(Continued on Next Page)

(Continued)

smoke over mesquite wood, if possible; baste chicken frequently with the barbecue sauce, turning the chicken periodically. Cook chicken 8 to 10 minutes per side. Any leftover barbecue sauce keeps well under refrigeration.

Savory Oven Fried Chicken

1 egg

½ cup milk

2 cups Cornflake crumbs

1 teaspoon seasoned salt

1 teaspoon Beau Monde seasoning

1 teaspoon parsley flakes

1 teaspoon dehydrated minced onion

½ teaspoon black pepper

¼ teaspoon garlic powder

½ stick margarine

6 chicken breasts or 1 cut up fryer

In a small bowl, beat together the egg and milk. In another small bowl, combine and mix together the Cornflakes crumbs, seasoned salt, Beau Monde, parsley flakes, onions, black pepper and garlic powder. Melt the margarine in the microwave, in a 9 x 13 inch baking dish. Dip each breast in the egg-milk mixture and then coat thoroughly with the seasoned crumbs. Place chicken in the baking dish and bake uncovered at 325 degrees for 1 hour and 10 minutes, or until coating on the chicken is golden brown.

Southern Fried Chicken

1 chicken, cut up
Salt
Pepper
2 eggs, beaten
2 tablespoons cream
Flour
Oil or shortening

Gravy:
3 tablespoons flour
½ teaspoon salt
½ teaspoon pepper
1½ cups whole milk

Salt and pepper each piece of chicken. Add cream to the beaten eggs and dip chicken into egg mixture and roll in the flour, coating chicken well. Heat about ¼ inch oil or shortening in a heavy skillet; brown chicken on both sides. Lower heat and cook until tender, about 25 minutes. For gravy, remove chicken from the skillet and add the 3 tablespoons flour, salt and pepper. Stir and turn burner to high heat. Add milk and cook, stirring until gravy thickens. Serve hot.

Mother knows best. — BCJ

Spicy Pepper Steak

1½ to 2 pounds lean sirloin or round steak,
sliced into thin strips
2 tablespoons oil
1 teaspoon garlic powder
¾ teaspoon ground ginger
1 teaspoon seasoned salt
½ teaspoon black pepper
3 green bell peppers, cut into chunks
1 onion, chopped
1 cup sliced celery
¼ cup soy sauce
1 teaspoon sugar
1 (14 ounce) can beef broth
2 tablespoons cornstarch
1 (4 ounce) can sliced mushrooms, drained
1 (10 ounce) can tomatoes and green chilies
Cooked rice or noodles

Cut steak in very thin strips (it will slice easier if frozen for an hour or so). Heat oil in a large skillet or roaster and brown steak; add garlic, ginger, seasoned salt and pepper. Remove meat and sauté green peppers, onion and celery for about 3 minutes. Add steak back to skillet or roaster; add soy sauce, sugar, beef broth, corn starch (which has been dissolved in a little cold water), mushrooms and tomatoes and green chilies. Bring ingredients to a boil and simmer about 30 minutes. (or you could put all this in a 3 quart casserole and cook it in a 350 degree oven for about 40 minutes. Serve over rice or noodles. Serves 10 to 12.

Smothered Steak

1½ pounds beef round or sirloin steak, about ¾ inch thick
Salt
Pepper
⅓ cup flour
3 tablespoons oil
3 medium onions, sliced
1 (10 ounce) can beef broth
1 tablespoon lemon juice
1 teaspoon garlic powder
¼ teaspoon dried thyme
½ teaspoon summer savory

Cut meat into serving sized pieces. Salt and pepper steak pieces and dip in flour. Pound the flour into the steak with a meat tenderizer. In a large skillet, brown steak in the oil. Top with onion slices. In a medium bowl combine remaining ingredients. Pour over steak, bring to a boil; reduce heat to a simmer. Cover and cook slowly for 1 hour. Check steak while cooking; you may need to add a little water. Serves 6 to 8.

Steak and Gravy

1 to 1½ pounds round steak, tenderized
Pepper
Flour
Oil
1 can golden cream of mushroom soup
1½ cans milk
1 package onion soup mix
1 (4 ounce) can mushrooms, undrained

Trim off any fat from steak; season with plenty of pepper. Cut

(Continued on Next Page)

(Continued)

steak in serving size pieces and dip each piece in flour, coating well. Brown in a large skillet in a little bit of oil. Place steak pieces in a Pam sprayed 9 x 13 inch glass baking dish. In the same skillet, combine mushroom soup, milk, onion soup mix and mushrooms. Blend and pour over steak pieces. Cover with foil and cook in a 350 degree oven for 1 hour. Serves 4 to 6.

Round Steak Casserole

2 pounds lean round steak, tenderized
Seasoned salt
Seasoned pepper
2 tablespoons oil
1 onion, chopped
1 cup uncooked rice
1 (14½ ounce) can beef broth
1 (14½ ounce) can water, plus ¼ cup
2 tablespoons Worcestershire
1 bell pepper, chopped
1 (4 ounce) can chopped green chilies (optional)
1 (2 ounce) jar sliced pimento

Trim fat off edges of steak and cut into serving size pieces. Season with seasoned salt and pepper. Pour oil in a very large (12 inch) skillet. (Must hold at least 3 quarts.) Brown steak on both sides in skillet. Pour over the steak, the onion, rice, beef broth, water, Worcestershire, bell pepper, green chilies and pimento. Stir slightly to mix ingredients and bring to a boil. Reduce heat to a low simmer. Cover. Simmer, covered for 35 minutes. Serves 8.

Corned Beef Supper

2 tomatoes, chopped
1 avocado, diced
3 chopped green onions
1 (3-ounce) can sliced ripe olives
1 (2-ounce) jar chopped pimentos
2 cups grated Cheddar cheese
1 (8-ounce) bag corn chips, slightly crushed
Catalina salad dressing
4 to 5 pound corned beef brisket
4 large potatoes, peeled and quartered
6 carrots, peeled and halved
1 head cabbage

Place corned beef in roaster, cover with water. Bring to a boil. Turn heat down and simmer 3 hours, adding water if necessary. Add potatoes and carrots. Cut cabbage into eighths and lay over top of potatoes, carrots and brisket. Bring to a boil; turn heat down and cook another 30 to 40 minutes, until vegetables are done. Slice corned beef across the grain. Serves 8. Leftover corned beef is good on sandwiches.

Chicken Fried Veal Steaks

½ cup milk
1 egg
¾ cup flour
½ teaspoon salt
¼ teaspoon black pepper
4 veal cutlets
Oil

In a small bowl, beat together the milk and egg. In another
(Continued on Next Page)

(Continued)

small flat bowl, mix together the flour, salt and pepper. First coat each cutlet with the seasoned flour, then dip in the milk-egg mixture and finally, coat each cutlet a second time in the seasoned flour. When coating the cutlet with the flour, press the flour into the cutlet so it will adhere to the surface of the cutlet. Deep fat fry in oil. Drain on paper towel and serve while hot.

Marvelous Meat Loaf

1 pound ground turkey
1 pound ground beef
2 eggs
1 envelope onion soup mix
¼ cup catsup
¼ cup minced bell pepper
½ cup sour cream
½ teaspoon garlic powder
½ teaspoon pepper
2 teaspoons Worcestershire
1 cup crushed crackers

Topping:
1¼ cups catsup
1 cup packed brown sugar
3 tablespoons Dijon mustard
Several shakes Tabasco

In a large mixing bowl, combine all meat loaf ingredients and mix well. Place meat mixture on a greased 9 x 13 inch baking pan and shape it like a loaf. Make it about the size of a loaf pan only with rounded corners. While meat is cooking, mix the topping in a medium saucepan and heat. Serve the topping for meat loaf separately in a gravy boat. Serves 8.

Lone Star Chicken-Fried Steak and Gravy

2 pounds round steak, tenderized
1¼ cups flour
1 teaspoon salt
Seasoned pepper
2 eggs, slightly beaten
½ cup milk
Oil

Cream gravy:
6 to 8 tablespoons pan grease or bacon drippings
6 tablespoons flour
3 cups milk
½ teaspoon salt
¼ teaspoon pepper.

Trim steak and cut into 6 to 8 pieces. Combine flour, salt and pepper and dredge all steak pieces in flour mixture until lightly coated. Combine eggs and milk. Dip steak into egg mixture and dredge again in flour, getting plenty of flour mashed into steak. Heat ½ inch oil in a heavy skillet and fry steak pieces until golden brown. To make gravy, remove steaks to warm oven, retaining drippings (bacon drippings make better gravy if you happen to have it). Add flour. Cook and stir until flour only begins to brown. Add milk and stir until thickened. Season with salt and pepper and serve in a bowl to cover steaks or mashed potatoes. This is a true Texas tradition!

Fry chicken this way too!

Slow Cook Brisket

1 large trimmed brisket
Seasoned salt
Seasoned pepper
Garlic powder
1 package onion soup mix
½ cup Worcestershire sauce

Preheat oven to 350 degrees. Generously sprinkle brisket with seasoned salt, seasoned pepper, garlic powder, and onion soup mix. Place brisket in an oven cooking bag (turkey size). Pour Worcestershire in bag and fasten. Bake at 350 degrees for 1 hour, reduce heat to 250 degrees and cook 1 hour per pound of meat.

Baked Barbecued Brisket

1 cup bottled barbecue sauce
½ cup water
½ onion, chopped
¼ cup liquid smoke
¼ cup Worcestershire
1 tablespoon garlic powder
2 teaspoons celery salt
2 teaspoons seasoned salt
2 teaspoons lemon pepper
1 teaspoon salt
5 to 6 pound beef brisket, well trimmed

In the bottom of a large baking dish like a Dutch oven, place all the ingredients except the brisket and stir. Add the brisket, fat side up. Spoon up some of the seasonings and drizzle over top of brisket. Seal with lid or foil and bake at 300 degrees for 5 hours. After brisket is done, let brisket set at room temperature for about 10 minutes. Slice as thin as possible across the grain.

Chuckwagon Barbecue

5 to 7 pound trimmed beef brisket
1 (4 ounce) bottle liquid smoke
½ teaspoon garlic salt
½ teaspoon onion salt
½ teaspoon celery salt
1 teaspoon seasoned pepper

Barbecue Sauce:
1 (16-ounce) bottle catsup
½ cup packed brown sugar
1 teaspoon prepared mustard
1½ teaspoons garlic powder
2 tablespoons Worcestershire
⅛ teaspoon cayenne pepper
¼ cup vinegar

Place brisket in a large baking pan and coat generously with the liquid smoke. Sprinkle spices over brisket and cover with foil and refrigerate overnight. Next day, pour off about ¾ of the liquid smoke. Combine all barbecue sauce ingredients and pour over brisket. Cook at 350 degrees for 1 hour; then lower heat to 275 degrees and cook for about 5 more hours. Let brisket cool at least 2 hours before slicing. The barbecue sauce will be thin so put it in a saucepan and boil about 15 minutes and it will be thick enough to serve over brisket.

Best Pot Roast

4 to 5 pound boneless rump roast
Seasoned salt
Seasoned pepper
Garlic powder
2 cups water
6 medium potatoes, peeled and cut in quarters
8 carrots, peeled and cut in quarters
3 onions, peeled and quartered

Gravy:
3 tablespoons cornstarch
¾ cup water
½ teaspoon pepper
½ teaspoon salt

Set roast in roasting pan with lid and sprinkle liberally with salt, pepper and garlic powder. Add 2 cups water and cook at 375 degrees for about 30 minutes. Turn heat down to 325 degrees and cook for about 3 hours. Add potatoes, carrots and onions. Cook another 35 to 40 minutes. To make gravy: lift the roast out of roaster and place on serving platter. Place potatoes, carrots and onion around roast. Combine cornstarch and ¼ cup water and add to juices left in roaster. Add pepper and salt. Cook on high on top of stove until gravy has thickened, stirring constantly. Serve in gravy boat with roast and vegetables. Serves 8.

Impossible Taco Pie

1 pound ground beef
½ cup chopped onion
1 envelope taco seasoning mix
1 (4 ounce) can chopped green chilies
1¼ cups milk
¾ cup biscuit mix
3 eggs

Topping:
1½ cups grated Cheddar cheese
Sour cream
Picante sauce

In a large skillet, brown ground beef and onion; drain off any fat. Stir in seasoning mix and green chilies. Spread in a greased 10 inch quiche dish or a 10 inch pie plate. Beat milk, biscuit mix and eggs together until smooth (about 1 minute with an electric mixer). Pour into pie plate with meat and bake 25 minutes at 400 degrees. Take out of oven and sprinkle with cheese. Return to oven and cook 5 to 8 minutes longer. Cool 5 minutes before slicing. Serve with a dab of sour cream and picante sauce. Serves 8.

Tex Mex Supper Salad

1 pound ground beef
1 large onion, chopped
1 (16-ounce) can red kidney beans, rinsed and drained
1½ teaspoons cumin
½ teaspoon garlic powder
½ teaspoon salt
1 cup water
½ to ¾ head lettuce, torn in bite size pieces

(Continued on Next Page)

(Continued)

In a skillet, sauté beef and onions. Drain off grease and add beans, spices and water and simmer until water is cooked out. In a large serving bowl, combine lettuce, tomatoes, avocado, onions, olives and pimentos. When ready to serve add warm beef mixture, cheese, chips, dressing and toss. Serve immediately. Serves 8.

Enchilada Casserole

1½ pounds ground beef
Salt and pepper
1 package taco seasoning mix
1¼ cups water
Oil
8 flour or corn tortillas
1 cup grated Cheddar cheese
1 (10-ounce) can enchilada sauce
1 (10 ounce) can green chilies
1 cup sour cream
1½ cups grated Monterey Jack cheese

Brown beef in skillet with salt and pepper and drain grease. Add taco seasoning mix and water to beef and simmer 5 minutes. In another skillet, heat oil until hot. Cook tortillas, one at a time until soft and limp, about 5 to 10 seconds on each side. Drain on paper towels. Spoon ⅓ cup meat mixture in center of tortilla. Sprinkle with small amount of Cheddar cheese and roll up and place seam side down into greased 9 x 13 baking dish. After filling all tortillas, add enchilada sauce and green chilies to remaining meat mixture. Spoon over tortillas. Cover and bake at 350 degrees for about 30 minutes. Uncover, spread sour cream over tortillas and sprinkle remaining cheese over all. Return to oven to heat sour cream and to melt cheese, about 5 to 10 minutes.

Super Spaghetti Pie

6 ounces spaghetti, cooked and drained
⅓ cup Parmesan cheese
1 egg, beaten
1 tablespoon margarine, melted
1 cup small curd cottage cheese
½ pound ground beef
½ pound sausage
½ cup chopped onion
1 (15-ounce) can tomato sauce
1 teaspoon garlic powder
1 tablespoon sugar
½ teaspoon salt
½ teaspoon seasoned pepper
1 teaspoon oregano
½ cup mozzarella cheese

While spaghetti is still warm, mix spaghetti, Parmesan cheese, egg and margarine in large bowl. Pour into a well greased 10" pie plate and pat mixture up and around sides with a spoon to form a crust. Put cottage cheese over spaghetti layer. In skillet, brown ground meat, sausage and onion. Drain off fat and add tomato sauce and seasonings. Simmer 10 minutes. Spoon meat mixture on top of cottage cheese. Bake at 350 degrees for 30 minutes. Arrange mozzarella on top and return to oven until cheese melts. This can be made ahead and placed in refrigerator until ready to cook. Serves 8.

Easy Lasagna

1 pound lean ground beef
1 onion, chopped
1 pound mozzarella cheese, grated
2 cups water
1 (15 ounce) can tomato sauce
1 (6 ounce) can tomato paste
2 tablespoons Worcestershire
1 tablespoon Italian herb seasoning
2 teaspoons parsley flakes
1 teaspoon salt
1 teaspoon sugar
¾ teaspoon garlic powder
½ teaspoon black pepper
8 ounces uncooked lasagna noodles
Grated parmesan cheese

In a roaster, brown the ground beef and onions. Add all remaining ingredients to the meat, except the noodles and parmesan cheese. In the bottom of a 9 x 13 inch baking dish, put about 2 cups of the meat and tomato sauce and spread out evenly. Add a layer of uncooked noodles. Top with another 2 cups sauce, another layer of noodles and cover the second layer of noodles with remaining sauce. Sprinkle top with lots of parmesan cheese. Cover casserole with foil and bake in a preheated 350 degree oven for 1 hour. Remove lasagna from oven and let set for 30 minutes before uncovering and serving. Before serving, sprinkle more Parmesan cheese over top. Can be made ahead of time; cooked, then frozen.

Chili Relleno Casserole

1 pound lean ground beef
1 bell pepper, chopped
1 onion, chopped
1 (4 ounce) can chopped green chilies
1 teaspoon oregano
1 teaspoon dried cilantro leaves
½ teaspoon garlic powder
½ teaspoon salt
½ teaspoon pepper
1 (7 ounce) can whole green chilies*
1½ cups grated Monterey Jack cheese
1½ cups grated sharp Cheddar cheese
3 large eggs
1 tablespoon flour
1 cup half and half or Milnot

In a skillet, brown meat with the bell pepper, onion, the 4 ounce can of green chilies, oregano, cilantro, garlic powder, salt and pepper. Seed whole chili peppers and spread on the bottom of a greased 9 x 13 inch baking dish. Cover with meat mixture and sprinkle with cheeses. Combine eggs and flour, beat with fork until fluffy. Add half and half; mix and pour over top of meat in casserole. Bake in a 350 degree oven for 30 to 35 minutes or until it is lightly browned. *You could use the chopped green chilies instead of the whole green chilies.

Texas Fajitas

2 pounds skirt steak or 6 chicken breasts, boned and skinned
Flour tortillas

Filling for Fajitas:
Salsa
Guacamole
Grilled onions
Chopped tomatoes
Grated cheese
Sour cream

Marinade:
1 cup picante sauce
1 cup bottled Italian dressing
2 tablespoons lemon juice
2 tablespoons chopped green onions
1 teaspoon garlic powder
1 teaspoon black pepper
1 teaspoon celery salt

Combine all marinade ingredients and mix well. Remove any fat from meat and wipe dry with paper towels. Place meat in a shallow dish and pour marinade over meat. Marinade overnight or at least 6 hours, in refrigerator. Drain liquid and broil over hot charcoal. Cut meat diagonally. Place a few strips of the meat on a heated flour tortilla and your choice of the fillings; then roll and eat!

Beef-Kebobs

2 to 2½ pounds sirloin steak
Fresh mushrooms
Bell peppers
Tiny onions
Cherry tomatoes

Marinade:
1 cup red wine
2 teaspoons Worcestershire
2 teaspoons garlic powder
1 cup oil
4 tablespoons catsup
2 teaspoons sugar
1 teaspoon salt
1 teaspoon monosodium glutamate
2 tablespoons vinegar
1 teaspoon marjoram
1 teaspoon rosemary
½ teaspoon seasoned pepper

Cut meat into 1½ to 2 inch chunks. Cut peppers into bite size pieces. Mix all ingredients of marinade together. Marinate steak pieces for 3 to 4 hours. Alternate meat, mushrooms, peppers, onions and cherry tomatoes on skewers. Cook over charcoal, turning on all sides, basting frequently with remaining marinade. Serves 8.

Swiss Steak

1 to 1½ pounds well trimmed, tenderized boneless round steak
Salt and pepper
Flour
Oil
2 onions, chopped
5 carrots, sliced
¾ teaspoon garlic powder
1 (16 ounce) can tomatoes, coarsely chopped
¾ cup picante sauce
½ cup water
2 teaspoons instant beef bouillon
1 tablespoon dried cilantro
1 teaspoon salt

Preheat oven to 325 degrees. Cut meat into serving size pieces; sprinkle with salt and pepper. Dredge in flour, coating well. Heat oil in large skillet and brown meat on both sides. Remove steak to a 9 x 13 inch baking dish. Cover with onions and carrots. Using the same skillet, combine garlic, tomatoes, picante sauce, water, beef bouillon, cilantro and salt. Heat and stir just to boiling point. Pour over steak, onions and carrots. Cook, covered for 1 hour. Serves 8. This dish can be made ahead and reheated just before serving.

Pineapple Glazed Ham

7 to 9 pound butt end ham (half cooked)
Whole cloves
1 (14 ounce) can chunk pineapple (save juice)
Maraschino cherries (optional)

Sauce:

1 cup red wine or cooking wine
1 cup packed brown sugar
A scant tablespoon cut up crystallized ginger
1½ teaspoons Dijon mustard
1 (8 ounce) can crushed pineapple

Stick LOTS of whole cloves on the outside of ham. With toothpicks stick the pineapple chunks in the ham and a cherry on top of the pineapple chunk, if you like. In a saucepan, combine the brown sugar, crystallized ginger, mustard, crushed pineapple and the juice from the chunk pineapple. Bring to a boil. Then turn off heat. Place ham in a roasting pan. Pour the hot sauce over the ham. Cook in a 350 degree preheated oven for 10 to 15 minutes per pound. Baste with the sauce every 20 minutes.

Saucy Ham Loaf

1 pound ham, ground
½ pound beef, ground
½ pound pork, ground
2 eggs
1 cup bread or cracker crumbs
2 teaspoons Worcestershire
1 small can evaporated milk
3 tablespoons chili sauce
1 teaspoon seasoned salt
1 teaspoon seasoned pepper
Bacon to strip top of loaf, optional

Sweet and Hot Mustard:

4 ounces Coleman's dry mustard
1 cup vinegar
3 eggs, beaten
1 cup sugar

Have butcher grind the three meats together. Mix all ingredients except bacon and sweet and hot mustard sauce ingredients. Form into a loaf in a 9 x 13 inch baking pan. Strip bacon on top and bake for 1 hour at 350 degrees. To make sweet and hot mustard: mix mustard and vinegar until smooth and let stand., overnight. Add eggs and sugar and cook in double boiler, stirring constantly 8-10 minute's or until it coats the spoon. Let cool and store in covered jars in refrigerator. Serve with ham loaf. Sweet and hot mustard is also wonderful on sandwiches too.

We've kept this old family recipe for more than 50 years.

239

Apricot Baked Ham

1 (12 to 20 pound) whole ham, fully cooked, bone-in
Whole cloves
2 tablespoons dry mustard
1¼ cups apricot jam
1¼ cups packed light brown sugar

Preheat oven to 450 degrees. Trim skin and excess fat from ham. Place ham on a rack in a large roasting pan. Insert cloves in ham every inch or so. Be sure to push cloves into the ham surface as far as they will go. Combine the dry mustard and the jam. Spread over entire surface of the ham. Pat the brown sugar over the jam mixture. Reduce heat to 325 degrees. Bake uncovered at 15 minutes per pound. The sugary crust that forms on the ham keeps the juices in. When ham is done, remove from oven and let ham set about 20 minutes before carving.

I usually buy a 10 to 12 pound "butt" end half a ham. And this crusty recipe makes it delicious!

Pork Loin with Apricot Glaze

1 (3 ½ to 4 pound) center-cut pork loin
1 tablespoon olive oil
Seasoned pepper
1 teaspoon dried rosemary
1 cup dry white wine (or cooking wine)
1 cup water
1½ cups apricot preserves

Rub pork loin with olive oil and sprinkle lots of seasoned pepper and rosemary over roast. Place loin in a shallow roasting pan. Pour wine and water into the bottom of the roasting pan. Roast in a 350 degree preheated oven for 1 hour. Remove pan from oven and spoon about one cup of pan

(Continued on Next Page)

240

(Continued)

drippings into a small bowl. Add the apricot preserves and mix well. Pour mixture over meat (turn oven down to 325 degrees) and return to the oven. Continue roasting for another hour, basting 2 to 3 times with pan drippings. Let meat rest at least 15 minutes before slicing. To cook the day before, cook as directed and let roast cool. Take roast out of drippings and place in a glass baking dish and slice. Put drippings in a separate container. Refrigerate both. When ready to serve, heat the drippings and pour over roast. Warm in a 350 degree oven for about 20 minutes.

Perfect Grilled Pork Tenderloin

2 pork tenderloins

Marinade:

⅔ cup soy sauce
⅔ cup oil
2 heaping tablespoons crystallized ginger, chopped very fine
2 tablespoons real lime juice
1 teaspoon garlic powder
2 tablespoons minced onion

Combine all ingredients of the marinade and pour into a large baggie; add the pork tenderloins and seal. Marinate 24 to 36 hours. When ready to serve, cook over charcoal about 45 minutes, occasionally basting with remaining marinade. Serves 6 to 8.

(When my Dad's 8-year-old granddaughter asked what he was cooking one dark and stormy night, he told her this was giraffe tongue. — SJ)
A terrific combination with this pork dish is Creamy Mashed Potatoes on page 175 and the Cauliflower and Broccoli Salad on page 119. Try it.

Sweet and Sour Pork Loin Roast

4 to 5 pound pork loin roast
Seasoned salt and pepper
Oil
½ cup water
1 (12 ounce) bottle chili sauce
1 (12 ounce) jar apricot preserves
1 (20 ounce) can chunk pineapple
2 bell peppers, sliced

Season roast with seasoned salt and pepper and brown in a little oil in a Dutch oven roaster. Add water to pan; cover and bake for 1 hour at 325 degrees. Mix together the chili sauce and apricot preserves and pour over roast. Lower oven to 250 degrees and cook another 2 hours. Add pineapple and bell pepper and cook another 15 minutes. Serves 8.

Ginger Baby Back Ribs

1 tablespoon margarine
1 onion, chopped
1 cup apricot preserves
¼ cup soy sauce
4 tablespoons honey
3 tablespoons red wine
1 tablespoon fresh grated ginger
1 tablespoon dried orange peel
4 to 5 pounds Baby Back Pork Ribs

Preheat oven to 375 degrees. Melt the margarine in a saucepan and cook onion until tender, but not brown. Add apricot preserves, soy sauce, honey, wine, ginger and orange peel. Cook, stiffing constantly until heated thoroughly. Place ribs in a

(Continued on Next Page)

(Continued)
large baking pan. Pour preserve mixture over the ribs. Cover and bake for 30 minutes; then reduce heat to 275 degrees and bake 3 to 3½ hours, until rib meat is tender. (If the ribs have not browned a little, remove cover and bake another 15 minutes, until they are pretty and brown.) The ribs will be delicious and practically fall off the bones! Serves 6 to 8.

Pork Chop Cheddar Bake

8 pork chops
1 can cream of mushroom soup
1¼ cups water
1 cup uncooked rice
1½ cups grated Cheddar cheese, divided
¼ cup minced onion
¼ cup chopped bell pepper
1 (4 ounce) can sliced mushrooms, drained
1 can French fried onions

In a large skillet, brown pork chops lightly. Drain and place in a greased 9 x 13 inch pyrex baking dish. In the same skillet, combine the soup, water, rice, ¼ cup cheese, onion, bell pepper and mushrooms; mix well. Pour over pork chops. Cover with foil and bake at 325 degrees for 1 hour and 10 minutes. Uncover and top with remaining cheese and French fried onions. Return to oven until cheese melts.

Pork Chops and Apples

6 thick cut pork chops
Flour
Oil
3 baking apples

Dip pork chops in flour and coat well. In a skillet, brown pork chops in oil. Place in a 9 x 13 inch greased casserole. Add about ⅓ cup water to casserole. Cook, covered at 325 degrees for about 45 minutes. Peel, half and seed apples. Place ½ apple on top of each pork chop. Return to oven for 5 to 10 minutes. (Don't overcook apples.)

These pork chops just melt in your mouth!

Herbed Baked Salmon

1½ pounds salmon fillets, skin intact
¾ cup mayonnaise
¾ cup freshly grated Parmesan cheese
1 bunch green onions, chopped
1 tablespoon chopped fresh parsley
1 tablespoon chopped fresh basil
1 tablespoon freshly chopped thyme
3 tablespoons minced red bell pepper
Juice of ½ lemon
½ teaspoon salt
¼ tablespoon black pepper
A scant ⅛ teaspoon cayenne pepper

Preheat oven to 350 degrees. Spray a shallow baking dish with Pam and warm oven. Combine mayonnaise, Parmesan, green onion, parsley, basil, thyme, bell pepper, lemon juice, salt, black

(Continued on Next Page)

(Continued)

pepper and cayenne pepper in a medium size bowl. Place salmon, skin side down on dish. Spread mayonnaise-herb mixture over salmon to within ½ inch of edges. Bake 20 to 25 minutes or just until flaky. Do not overcook.

Blackened Fillets

3 teaspoons paprika

1 teaspoon garlic powder

1 teaspoon onion powder

2 teaspoons salt

1 teaspoon crushed red pepper

1 teaspoon white pepper

1 teaspoon black pepper

½ teaspoon thyme

½ teaspoon oregano

4 (¼ inch thick) fish fillets

1 stick margarine, melted

On a square of waxed paper, mix together the paprika, garlic and onion powder, salt, the 3 peppers, thyme and oregano. This is your blackening mixture. Brush the fish fillets with the melted margarine, coating both sides. Generously sprinkle both sides of the fish with the blackened mixture, coating both sides well. Heat a large cast-iron skillet over very high heat until it is beyond the smoking stage. The skillet cannot be too hot for this dish. Place about a tablespoon of the margarine in skillet. Place the blackened fillet in the heated skillet, add 1 teaspoon melted margarine on top of each fillet. Cook fish 2 minutes per side. Serve immediately.

Tequila-Lime Shrimp

½ stick margarine
2 tablespoons olive oil
½ teaspoon garlic powder
1½ pounds medium shrimp, shelled and deveined
3 tablespoons tequila
3 tablespoons lime juice
½ teaspoon salt
½ teaspoon chili powder
¼ teaspoon seasoned salt
¼ teaspoon black pepper
½ teaspoon ground coriander
1 tablespoon dried cilantro
Hot cooked rice

Pat shrimp dry with paper towel. Heat margarine and oil in a large skillet over medium heat. Add garlic powder and shrimp; cook about 2 minutes, stirring occasionally. Stir in tequila, lime juice, salt, chili powder, seasoned salt, pepper and coriander. Cook 2 minutes more (most of the liquid will be gone); shrimp should be pink and glazed. Add the cilantro. Serve over hot cooked rice.

With a green salad, this makes a great light and delicious lunch!

Crab and Angel Hair Pasta

1 stick margarine
½ onion, finely chopped
1 bell pepper, chopped
1 teaspoon dried summer savory
1 teaspoon dried parsley flakes
1 teaspoon dried basil
½ teaspoon celery salt
1 teaspoon rosemary
½ teaspoon lemon pepper
½ teaspoon salt
2 (16 ounce) cans diced tomato
1 (16 ounce) can Italian style stewed tomatoes
½ cup dry white wine (optional)
1 pound crabmeat (or lobster)
1 pound angel hair pasta, cooked
Freshly grated Parmesan cheese

In a large saucepan, melt margarine and sauté onion and bell pepper. Stir in all seasonings and the tomatoes; heat to a boil. Add wine; simmer for 5 minutes. Add crabmeat and simmer 2 minutes. Place warm pasta in a serving dish and top with crab mixture. Serve with the Parmesan cheese. Serves 6 to 8.

Salmon Croquettes

1 (15 ounce) can salmon
½ teaspoon seasoned salt
½ teaspoon black pepper
¼ cup shrimp cocktail sauce or chili sauce
½ (10¾ ounce) can cream of chicken soup*
1 egg
½ onion, finely chopped
Several dashes of Tabasco
1⅓ cups cracker crumbs
Flour
Oil

Drain salmon well in a colander. Remove the skin and the little back bones. Place salmon in mixing bowl and add the seasoned salt, pepper, cocktail sauce, soup, egg, onion, Tabasco and cracker crumbs. Mix well. Pat croquettes into shapes like a triangle-shaped log and roll in flour. Make 10 to 12 logs. Pour just enough oil in a large skillet, to cover the bottom; turn to medium heat. Place croquettes in skillet and fry. Turn twice so you have 3 sides that brown. You might add an extra tablespoon oil halfway through cooking. It will take about 15 minutes to fry on 3 sides. (Of course you could deep fry croquettes if you want.) *Use the remaining cream of chicken soup by diluting with equal parts of milk and have a cup of soup as an appetizer.

*This was a regular when the kids were growing up.
I've learned in the last few years that people in various parts
of the country make flat patties. We had quite a
discussion about which was the "right" way.*

Say please and thank you.

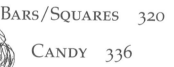

Outa Sight Pie

1 can sweetened condensed milk
1 can lemon pie filling
1 (20 ounce) can crushed pineapple, well drained
1 (8 ounce) carton Cool Whip
2 cookie flavored ready pie crusts

In a large mixing bowl, combine the condensed milk, lemon pie filling and the pineapple; mix well. Fold in Cool Whip. Pour into 2 pie crusts. Refrigerate several hours.

Eat one pie and freeze the other.

Peach Mousse Pie

9 inch graham cracker pie crust (or the cookie crust)
1 (16 ounce) package frozen peach slices, thawed
1 cup sugar
1 envelope unflavored gelatin
1/8 teaspoon ground nutmeg
A few drops of yellow and red food coloring
3/4 of a 12 ounce carton of Cool Whip
Nectarine slices for decoration

Place peaches in blender and process until peaches are smooth. Place in a saucepan and bring to boiling point, stirring constantly. Set off burner. Stir together the sugar, gelatin and nutmeg and stir into hot puree; stirring until sugar and gelatin are dissolved. Pour gelatin mixture into large mixing bowl. Place in deep freeze just until mixture mounds-stirring occasionally (about 20 minutes). Beat mixture at high speed about 5 minutes until mixture becomes light and fluffy. Add coloring. Fold in Cool Whip and pour into pie crust.

Really light and delicious!

White Chocolate Pie

4 ounces white chocolate
20 large marshmallows
½ cup milk
1 (8 ounce) carton Cool Whip
⅔ cup chopped pecans
½ cup maraschino cherries, chopped, well-drained
9 inch graham cracker pie crust

Melt together in a double boiler the white chocolate, marshmallows and milk. Cool. Fold in Cool Whip, pecans and cherries. Pour into pie crust and freeze. Take out of freezer 15 minutes before serving.

Dream Pie

1 (8 ounce) package cream cheese, softened
1 (14 ounce) can sweetened condensed milk
1 (5.1 ounce) package vanilla instant pudding mix
½ cup water
1 (8 ounce) carton Cool Whip
2 graham cracker ready pie crusts
1 can strawberry pie filling*

In mixer bowl, beat together cream cheese and sweetened condensed milk until smooth. Add pudding mix and water; mix. Chill about 15 minutes. Fold in Cool Whip. Pour into 2 pie crusts and freeze. When ready to serve, take out of freezer and place in refrigerator about 45 minutes before slicing and serving. Spoon about ¼ cup of the pie filling on each slice of pie. *You could use any of the other pie fillings instead of strawberry. Variation: use 2 chocolate ready pie crusts. Pour 2 or 3 tablespoons chocolate ice cream topping over pie. Top with chocolate shavings

German Chocolate Pie

1 (4 ounce) package German sweet chocolate
1 stick margarine
1 (14½ ounce) can evaporated milk
1½ cups sugar
3 tablespoons cornstarch
⅛ teaspoon salt
2 eggs
1 teaspoon vanilla
1 (10 inch) pie crust, unbaked
1 (3½ ounce) can coconut
½ cup chopped pecans

Melt chocolate with margarine over low heat. Gradually blend in milk. In a mixing bowl mix sugar, cornstarch and salt thoroughly. Beat in eggs and vanilla. Gradually blend into chocolate mixture. Pour into pie crust. Combine coconut and pecans and sprinkle over filling. Bake at 350 degrees for 45 to 50 minutes. Filling will be soft but will set while cooling. Cool at least 4 hours before slicing.

Strawberry Cream Cheese Pie

1 (10 ounce) package frozen sweetened strawberries, thawed
2 (8 ounce) packages cream cheese, softened
⅔ cup powdered sugar
1 (8 ounce) carton Cool Whip
1 prepared chocolate crumb crust

Drain strawberries, reserving ¼ cup liquid. In a mixing bowl, combine cream cheese, reserved liquid, strawberries and sugar. Beat well. Fold in Cool Whip. Spoon into crust. Refrigerate overnight. Garnish with fresh strawberries.

Pecan Pie

2 tablespoons flour
3 tablespoons margarine, melted
3 eggs, beaten
⅔ cup sugar
1 cup corn syrup
1 teaspoon vanilla
1 cup chopped pecans
1 (9 inch) pie shell, unbaked

Preheat oven to 350 degrees. In mixing bowl, combine flour, margarine, eggs, sugar, corn syrup and vanilla; mix well. Place pecans in pie shell and pour egg mixture over pecans. Bake at 350 degrees for 10 minutes. Reduce heat to 275 degrees and bake 50 to 55 minutes or until center of pie is fairly firm. Variation: (1) Instead of vanilla, use 2 tablespoons Amaretto. (2) Add 1 teaspoon cinnamon and ¼ teaspoon nutmeg.

Birthday Pumpkin Chiffon Pie

1 envelope Knox gelatin
¼ cup cold water
2 eggs
1 ¼ cups sugar
1 ¼ cups canned pumpkin
⅔ cup milk
½ teaspoon ground ginger
½ teaspoon nutmeg
⅓ teaspoon cinnamon
½ teaspoon salt
1 (8 ounce) carton whipping cream
1 (9 inch) baked pie crust

Soften gelatin in cold water and set aside. With mixer, beat eggs about 3 minutes. Add the sugar, pumpkin, milk, spices and salt. Mix well. Pour this mixture into a large saucepan and cook in double boiler until custard consistency, stirring constantly. Mix in softened gelatin and dissolve in the hot pumpkin mixture. (Do not use Cool Whip). Pour into the baked pie crust and refrigerate several hours before slicing.

Original "chiffon" pies have the egg whites whipped and folded into the pie. But now "they" tell us that we should not eat the white or the yolk of an egg without cooking, so in this recipe, I have cooked the whole eggs and added whipped cream. It is delicious!

My daughter has a fall birthday and she decided when she was 10 to do away with the birthday cake. She liked Pumpkin Chiffon Pie better. (You can put candles on a pie, but she stopped the candle idea when she went off to college.)

This is the absolute best pumpkin pie in the world. I'm a pumpkin pie expert. I've been testing them for many years, but I'm not telling how many years and how many pies. — S.J.

Pumpkin Cream Pie

1 (8 ounce) package cream cheese, softened
2 cups powdered sugar
1 (8 ounce) carton Cool Whip
2 (6 ounce) butter flavored ready pie crusts
¼ cup milk
1 (5 ounce) package instant vanilla pudding
½ cup powdered sugar
1 (16 ounce) can pumpkin
1 teaspoon cinnamon
½ teaspoon ginger
¼ teaspoon cloves

In mixer bowl, combine cream cheese and 2 cups powdered sugar; beat until well combined. Fold in Cool Whip. Pour ½ cream cheese mixture in each pie crust. In the same mixing bowl, combine milk, instant pudding and ½ cup powdered sugar; beat until smooth. Fold in pumpkin, cinnamon, ginger and cloves. Spread ½ pumpkin mixture over both pies. Refrigerate 3 or 4 hours before serving. Eat one pie and freeze the other.

Strawberry Margarita Pie

60 vanilla wafers
1 stick margarine, melted
1 can sweetened condensed milk
2 tablespoons lime juice
¼ cup Tequila
⅓ cup Triple Sec
2 (10 ounce) packages sweetened strawberries, thawed, drained
1 (8 ounce) carton Cool Whip
Fresh strawberries for garnish

Crush vanilla wafers in food processor or crush in a baggie. Pour into a large springform pan. Pour in melted margarine; mix well. Pat down. In a large mixing bowl, combine sweetened condensed milk, lime juice, Tequila and Triple Sec. Stir until completely mixed. Add strawberries and Cool Whip; fold in. Pour into springform pan and freeze. Leave in freezer until ready to serve. Garnish with fresh strawberries. Serves 12.

Creamy Lemon Pie

1 (8 ounce) package cream cheese, softened
1 can sweetened condensed milk
¼ cup lemon juice
1 can lemon pie filling
1 (9 inch) graham cracker pie crust

In mixing bowl, cream cheese until creamy. Add sweetened condensed milk and lemon juice. Beat until mixture is very creamy. Fold in lemon pie filling; stirring well. Pour into pie crust. Refrigerate several hours before slicing and serving.

Lemony and creamy — a good combination!
This is one of my favorites.

Lemon Pecan Chess Pie

2 ¼ cups sugar
2 tablespoons flour
1 tablespoon cornmeal
4 eggs, lightly beaten
2 tablespoons grated lemon rind
¼ cup lemon juice
¾ cup chopped pecans
1 unbaked pie crust

Combine sugar, flour and cornmeal in a large bowl. Toss lightly. Add eggs, lemon rind and the lemon juice. Mix until smooth and thoroughly blended. Add pecans to mixture and pour into the pie crust. Tear off three 1½ inch strips of foil. Cover the crust with these strips (crimp a little where foil pieces come together); it will keep the crust from getting too brown. Bake at 400 degrees for 10 minutes. Turn oven temperature down to 325 degrees and bake 40 to 45 minutes or until center is not shaky.

Cinnamon Almond Pecan Pie

1 (9 inch) unbaked pie shell
⅔ cup sugar
1 tablespoon flour
2 ½ teaspoons cinnamon
4 eggs, lightly beaten
1 cup light corn syrup
2 tablespoons margarine, melted
1 tablespoon vanilla
1 ½ teaspoons almond extract
1 cup coarsely chopped pecans
½ cup slivered almonds

Stir together the sugar and flour. Add the cinnamon, eggs, corn syrup, margarine, vanilla and almond extract; mixing well. Stir in chopped pecans and slivered almonds. Pour filling into the pie shell. Tear off three 1½ inch strips of foil. Cover the crust with these strips (crimp a little where foil pieces come together); it will keep the crust from getting too brown. Bake 10 minutes at 400 degrees, then reduce heat to 325 degrees and bake 40 to 45 minutes more or until pie will just barely shake in center. Cool completely before serving.

A little change from the traditional pecan pie, but a good one!

Pistachio Lime Pie

2 cups vanilla wafer crumbs
¼ cup chopped pistachio nuts (or pecans)
¼ cup margarine, melted
1 (8 ounce) package cream cheese, softened
1 can sweetened condensed milk
¼ cup lime juice from concentrate
1 (3 ounce) package instant pistachio pudding mix
½ cup chopped pistachio nuts (or pecans)
1 (8 ounce) can crushed pineapple, undrained
1 (8 ounce) carton Cool Whip

Combine crumbs, ¼ cup nuts and margarine and press firmly on bottom of a 9 inch springform pan. Bake 8 to 10 minutes and cool. In a large mixing bowl, beat cheese until fluffy and gradually beat in sweetened condensed milk and then the lime juice and pudding mix and beat until smooth. Stir in ½ cup nuts and pineapple and fold in Cool Whip. Pour into the springform pan and chill overnight. Keep refrigerated.

A bridge club favorite!

Kahlua Pie

26 marshmallows
1 (13 ounce) can evaporated milk
1 package unflavored gelatin
¼ cup cold water
1 (8 ounce) carton whipping cream
½ cup Kahlua
1 (9 inch) chocolate cookie pie crust
Chocolate curls

In a saucepan, melt marshmallows in evaporated milk, using low to medium heat; stir constantly and do not let milk come to a boil. Remove from heat and add gelatin that has been dissolved in cold water. Chill until mixture becomes slightly thickened. Whip the cream and fold into marshmallow mixture. Mix in Kahlua. Pour into pie crust and garnish with chocolate curls. Chill overnight.

Peachy Ginger Cobbler

2 tablespoons cornstarch
2 tablespoons margarine
⅓ cup water
1½ cups sugar
¼ teaspoon cinnamon
3 cups fresh peaches, peeled and sliced
¼ cup chopped crystallized ginger (no substitutions)

Topping:
1 cup flour
½ cup sugar
½ cup packed brown sugar
¼ teaspoon salt
½ teaspoon baking powder
1 egg
½ stick margarine, melted
1 cup chopped pecans

In a saucepan, combine cornstarch, margarine, water, sugar and cinnamon. Heat, stirring constantly until mixture has thickened. Stir in peaches and crystallized ginger. Pour into a greased 8 x 12 inch baking dish. For topping, mix all ingredients together. Dot teaspoonfuls over peaches. Bake at 350 degrees for 40 to 45 minutes or until golden brown. Serves 8.

Apricot Cobbler

1 can apricot pie filling
1 (20 ounce) can crushed pineapple, undrained
1 cup chopped pecans
1 yellow cake mix
2 sticks margarine, melted
Cool Whip

Spray a 9 x 13 inch baking dish with Pam. Pour the apricot pie filling in the pan and spread out. Then spoon the crushed pineapple and juice over the pie filling. Sprinkle the pecans over the pineapple; then sprinkle the cake mix over the pecans. Pour the melted margarine over the cake mix and bake at 375 degrees for 40 minutes or until lightly brown and crunchy. To serve, top with Cool Whip. Serves 10.

A bridge partner had this recently and everybody gave this a
"blue ribbon". This is another one of those recipes that
*is really **quick and easy** plus really delicious.*

Blueberry Streusel Cobbler

1 (14 ounce) package frozen blueberries, thawed
1 can sweetened condensed milk
2 teaspoon grated lemon rind
1 ½ sticks margarine, softened
2 cups biscuit baking mix
⅔ cup firmly packed brown sugar
2 tablespoons margarine
¾ cup chopped pecans

Blueberry Sauce:
½ cup sugar
1 tablespoon cornstarch
½ teaspoon cinnamon
¼ teaspoon ground nutmeg
½ cup water
1 (14 ounce) package frozen blueberries, thawed
Vanilla ice cream

In a medium bowl, combine blueberries, sweetened condensed milk and rind. In a large bowl, cut the stick and a half of margarine into 1½ cups of the biscuit mix until crumbly. Add the blue berry mixture. Spread in a greased and floured 9 x 13 inch baking dish. In small bowl, combine remaining ½ cup biscuit mix and brown sugar. Cut in remaining 2 tablespoons margarine until crumbly. Add pecans. Sprinkle over cobbler. In a preheated 325 degrees oven, bake for 55 to 60 minutes (using a toothpick, test to be sure it is done). For the sauce: in a small saucepan, combine sugar, cornstarch, cinnamon and nutmeg. Gradually add ½ cup water. Cook and stir until thickened. Stir in blueberries. Serve a square of cobbler with a dip of ice cream on top; then pour blueberry sauce over all. Serves 12.

Blueberry Crumble

1 (13 ounce) box wild blueberry muffin mix
⅓ cup sugar
½ teaspoon cinnamon
½ stick margarine, melted
⅔ cup chopped pecans
1 (16 ounce) can blueberry pie filling
¼ cup sugar
1 teaspoon cinnamon

In a bowl, combine the muffin mix, sugar, cinnamon and melted margarine. Stir and mix until crumbly. Add pecans and mix. Set aside. Pour the blueberry pie filling into a Pam sprayed 7 x 11 inch glass baking dish. Pour the can of drained blueberries that comes in the mix over the top of pie filling. Sprinkle the sugar and cinnamon over top. Then crumble, with your hands, the muffin mixture over the top of the pie filling. Bake at 350 degrees for 35 minutes. To serve, hot or room temperature, top with a dip of vanilla ice cream. Serves 8.

Fruit Fajitas

1 can prepared fruit pie filling
10 small or 8 large flour tortillas
2 cups water
1½ cups sugar
1½ sticks margarine
1 teaspoon almond flavoring

Divide fruit equally on tortillas, roll up and place in a 9 x 13 baking dish. Mix together water, sugar and margarine in saucepan and bring to a boil. Add almond flavoring and pour over flour tortillas. Place in refrigerator and let soak 1 to 24 hours. Bake 350 degrees for 20 to 25 minutes until brown and bubbly.

Date Pecan Tarts

1 (8 ounce) package chopped dates
2½ cups milk
½ cup flour
1½ cups sugar
3 eggs
½ teaspoon salt
1 teaspoon vanilla
1 cup chopped pecans
8 tart shells, baked and cooled
1 (8 ounce) carton whipping cream
3 tablespoons powdered sugar

In a saucepan, cook dates, milk, flour and sugar until thick, stirring constantly. Add beaten eggs and salt. Cook this mixture about 5 minutes on medium heat; stirring constantly. Stir in vanilla and pecans. Pour into the tart shells. Cool. Whip cream and add powdered sugar. Top each tart with a heaping tablespoon of whipped cream.

This is an old-time favorite!

White Chocolate Cheesecake

2 cups graham cracker crumbs
1 cup finely chopped slivered almonds
4 tablespoons margarine, softened
8 ounces white chocolate
4 (8 ounces) packages cream cheese, softened
¾ cup sugar
5 eggs
2 tablespoons flour
1 teaspoon flour
1 teaspoon vanilla
Strawberries or raspberries
Sugar

Combine graham cracker crumbs, almonds and margarine in a bowl. Mix well and press into the bottom of a 10 inch springform pan. Melt white chocolate in a double boiler. Stir until smooth and remove from heat. In mixer bowl, beat the cream cheese until smooth and fluffy. Add sugar. Beat in eggs, one at a time. Add flour and vanilla. Mix until smooth. Fold in the melted white chocolate. Pour mixture over the graham cracker crust. Bake at 275 degrees for 60 minutes or until top is firm to the touch. Cool completely, cover and chill overnight. To serve, remove sides of the springform pan. Slice the strawberries (leave the raspberries whole) and sprinkle on a little sugar. Spoon about ¼ cup of fruit over a slice of cheesecake. You should get about 16 slices of cheesecake.

The best way to slice a cheesecake is to use a very sharp knife, cleaning after each slice; then dip it in water before slicing each piece.

Praline Cheesecake

1¼ cups graham cracker crumbs
4 tablespoons sugar
4 tablespoons margarine, melted
3 (8 ounce) packages cream cheese, softened
1¼ cups packed dark brown sugar
2 tablespoons flour
3 large eggs
2 teaspoons vanilla
½ cup finely chopped pecans halves
Maple syrup

Combine crumbs, sugar and margarine; press into the bottom of a 9 inch springform pan. Bake at 350 degrees for 10 minutes. In mixing bowl, combine cream cheese, brown sugar and flour, mixing at medium speed on electric mixer until well blended. Add eggs, one at a time, mixing well after each addition. Blend in vanilla and stir in chopped pecans. Pour over crust. Bake at 350 degrees for 50 to 55 minutes. Loosen cake from rim of pan, but cool before removing rim of pan. Chill. Place pecan halves around the edge of the cake (about 1 inch from the edge) about 1 inch apart. Then pour syrup over top of cheesecake. When you slice the cheesecake, you might want to pour another teaspoon of the syrup over each slice so some will run down sides of the slice.

Tropical Cheesecake

1¼ cups graham cracker crumbs
½ cup coconut
½ cup chopped pecans
2 tablespoons light brown sugar
½ stick margarine, melted
2 (8-ounce) packages cream cheese, softened
1 (14-ounce) can sweetened condensed milk
3 eggs
¼ cup frozen orange juice concentrate, thawed
1 teaspoon pineapple extract
1 can pineapple pie filling
1 cup sour cream

Combine crumbs, coconut, pecans, brown sugar and margarine. Press firmly on bottom of a 9 inch springform pan and set aside. In a large mixing bowl, beat cream cheese until fluffy. Gradually beat in condensed milk. Add eggs, juice concentrate and pineapple extract and mix well. Stir in ¾ cup of the pineapple pie filling. Pour into the prepared springform pan. Bake 1 hour at 300 degrees or until center is set. Spread top with sour cream and bake 5 minutes longer. Cool. Spread remaining pineapple pie filling over cheesecake and refrigerate.

1 stick *m*
½ cup Cris*co*
4 tablespoons coco*a*
1 cup water
½ cup buttermilk
2 eggs
1 teaspoon soda
1 teaspoon cinnamon
1 teaspoon vanilla

Icing:
1 stick margarine, melted
4 tablespoons cocoa
6 tablespoons milk
1 (16 ounce) box powdered sugar
1 teaspoon vanilla
1 cup chopped pecans

Combine flour and sugar in large mixer bowl. In a saucepan, combine margarine, Crisco, cocoa and the one cup of water; bring to a boil. Pour this mixture into the flour-sugar mixture and beat. Then add the buttermilk, eggs, soda, cinnamon and vanilla. Beat well. Pour into a greased and floured 10 x 15 inch baking dish. Bake 25 minutes at 375 degrees. For the icing, combine melted margarine, cocoa, milk, powdered sugar and vanilla. Stir until well mixed and add pecans. Pour icing over hot cake. Serves 15.

*Want a "chocolate fix **quick**" — this is it!*

Death by Chocolate

2 cups flour
2 cups sugar
...margarine

CAKES

...er the bottom of
...mixer bowl, mix
...beating well. Pour
...nut. In mixer bowl,
comb... ...nd powdered sugar;
whip to b... ...er. Bake at 350 degrees
for 40 to 42 min... ...r doneness with a cake
tester, as the cake wi... ...ven when it is done. The
icing sinks into the bottom a... ..., forming the white ribbon
inside. Makes a delicious and eas... ...ake to make.

*This is **easy** and very, very yummy.*

270

Red Devil Cake

2 cups sugar
2 cups flour
½ cup shortening
1 stick margarine
1 cup water
4 tablespoons cocoa
½ cup buttermilk
2 eggs, beaten
1 teaspoon soda
1 teaspoon vanilla

Icing:

1 stick margarine
4 tablespoons cocoa
6 tablespoons milk
1 (1 pound) box powdered sugar
1 teaspoon vanilla
1 cup chopped pecans
Several dashes red food coloring

Preheat oven to 350 degrees. In a large mixing bowl, combine sugar and flour. In a saucepan, bring to a boil the shortening, margarine, water and cocoa. Pour over flour mixture while still hot. Add buttermilk, beaten eggs, soda and vanilla. Beat well. Pour into a large 15 ½ x 10 ½ inch greased and floured pan. Bake for 20 to 25 minutes. Test for doneness with toothpick. While cake is baking, make icing. Bring to a boil the margarine, cocoa and milk. Remove from heat. Add powdered sugar. Mix well. Add pecans and red food coloring. Spread cake while both are still hot.

Chocolate Cherry Cake

1 milk chocolate cake mix
1 can cherry pie filling
3 eggs

Frosting:
5 tablespoons margarine
1¼ cups sugar
½ cup milk
1 (6 ounce) package chocolate chips

Combine cake mix, pie filling and eggs in mixing bowl. Mix by hand. Pour into a greased and floured 9 x 13 inch baking pan. Bake at 350 degrees for 35 to 40 minutes. Test cake for doneness with toothpick. When cake is done, combine margarine, sugar and milk in a medium saucepan. Bring to boiling point and boil 1 minute, stirring constantly. Add chocolate chips and stir until chips are melted. Pour over hot cake.

Scotch Cake

2 cups sugar
2 cups flour
1 stick margarine
½ cup Crisco
4 heaping tablespoons cocoa
1 cup water
½ cup buttermilk
4 eggs, beaten
1 teaspoon soda
1 teaspoon cinnamon
1 teaspoon vanilla
½ teaspoon salt

Frosting:
1 stick margarine, melted
4 tablespoons cocoa
6 tablespoons milk
1 box powdered sugar
1 teaspoon vanilla
1 cup chopped pecans
1 can flaked coconut

Blend flour and sugar together in a mixing bowl. In a saucepan, bring margarine, oil, cocoa and water to a boil and pour over flour and sugar mixture, beating well. Add buttermilk, eggs, soda, cinnamon, vanilla and salt. Mix well and pour into a greased and floured 9 x 13 inch pan and bake at 350 degrees for 40 to 45 minutes. Five minutes before cake is done combine margarine, cocoa, milk, powdered sugar and vanilla and mix well. Add pecans and coconut and mix. Spread on hot cake.

Turtle Cake

1 box German chocolate cake mix
1 stick margarine, softened
1½ cups water
½ cup oil
1 can sweetened condensed milk, divided
1 pound bag caramels
1 cup chopped pecans

Frosting:
1 stick margarine
3 tablespoons cocoa
6 tablespoons evaporated milk
1 box powdered sugar
1 teaspoon vanilla

Combine cake mix, margarine, water, oil and half the condensed milk. Pour half the batter into a greased and floured 9 x 13 inch pan and bake at 350 degrees for 20 minutes. Melt caramels and blend with the remaining condensed milk. Spread evenly over baked cake layer and sprinkle with pecans. Cover with remaining batter and bake an additional 20 to 25 minutes. For frosting, melt margarine in a saucepan and mix in cocoa and milk. Add powdered sugar and vanilla to mixture and blend well. Spread over cake. Serves 24.

Black Russian Cake

1 milk chocolate cake mix
½ cup oil
1 (3.9 ounce) package instant chocolate pudding mix
4 eggs, room temperature
⅔ cup strong brewed coffee
⅓ cup Kahlua
⅓ cup Créme de Cacao liqueur

Icing:
1½ cups powdered sugar
2 tablespoons margarine, melted
Enough Kahlua to make the icing spreadable

In mixer bowl, combine cake mix, oil, pudding mix, eggs, coffee and liqueurs. Beat for 4 to 5 minutes. Spoon into a greased and floured bundt pan. Bake at 350 degrees for 55 to 60 minutes. Test with toothpick for doneness. Cool. For the icing, combine the powdered sugar and melted margarine and spoon in, a little at a time, the Kahlua until you have a spreadable consistency but thin enough to run down sides. Serves 20. Better if you put a dip of vanilla ice cream on top!

Poppy Seed Cake

3 cups sugar
1¼ cups shortening
6 eggs
3 cups flour
¼ teaspoon soda
½ teaspoon salt
1 cup buttermilk
3 tablespoons poppy seeds
2 teaspoons almond extract
2 teaspoons vanilla
2 teaspoons butter flavoring

Glaze:

1½ cups powdered sugar
⅓ cup lemon juice
1 teaspoon vanilla
1 teaspoon almond extract

In a large mixing bowl, cream sugar and shortening until mixture is light and fluffy. Add eggs, one at a time, blending mixture well. Sift together flour, soda and salt. Alternately add dry ingredients and buttermilk to the sugar mixture. Add poppy seeds and flavorings and blend well. Pour into a greased and floured bundt pan. Cook at 325 degrees for 1 hour and 15 to 20 minutes. Test with toothpick for doneness. For the glaze, combine all ingredients and mix well. Pour over top of cooled cake and let some of the glaze run down the sides of the cake.

Chocolate Pound Cake

3 cups sugar
2 sticks butter, softened
½ cup shortening
5 eggs
3 cups flour
½ cup cocoa
½ teaspoon baking powder
¼ teaspoon salt
1 cup milk
1 teaspoon vanilla
Powdered sugar

Cream sugar, butter and shortening at medium speed of electric mixer. Add eggs, one at a time, beating well after each addition. Sift together flour, cocoa, baking powder and salt. Reduce mixer speed to low and add one half the dry ingredients, then the milk and vanilla, beating well after each addition. Last add the remaining flour, beating well. Pour into a greased and floured 10 inch bundt pan. Bake at 300 degrees for one hour and 20 minutes. Cool 10 minutes in pan. Turn on to rack or plate to cool. Sprinkle powdered sugar over top of the cake.

This is one of my favorites.

Double Chocolate Pound Cake

2 sticks margarine, softened
½ cup shortening
1 (3 ounce) package cream cheese, softened
3 cups sugar
2 teaspoons vanilla
5 large eggs
½ cup cocoa
3 cups flour
1 teaspoon baking powder
½ teaspoon salt
1 cup buttermilk
1 (6 ounce) package chocolate chips
Powdered sugar

Preheat oven to 325 degrees. In a large mixer bowl, cream together margarine, shortening, cream cheese and sugar. Beat at high speed for 5 minutes; add vanilla. Add eggs and beat well. In separate bowl mix together cocoa, flour, baking powder and salt. Add half dry ingredients to the batter, then the buttermilk, ending with remaining dry ingredients. Beat well after each addition. Fold in chocolate chips. Pour into a greased and floured 10 inch tube pan and bake 1 hour and 30 minutes. Test with toothpick for doneness. Let cake cool in pan for about 15 minutes; then turn onto cake plate; cook completely. Dust with sifted powdered sugar.

Peanut Butter Pound Cake

1 cup butter
2 cups sugar
1 cup packed light brown sugar
½ cup creamy peanut butter
5 eggs
1 tablespoon vanilla
3 cups flour
½ teaspoon baking powder
½ teaspoon baking soda
½ teaspoon salt
1 cup whipping cream

Frosting:
½ stick margarine, softened
3 to 4 tablespoons milk
⅓ cup creamy or chunky peanut butter
1 (16 ounce) box powdered sugar

Cream together the butter, sugars and peanut butter and beat until fluffy. Add eggs, one at a time, beating well after each addition. Add vanilla and blend. Sift together the dry ingredients and add alternately with whipping cream. Pour into a large greased and floured tube pan. Bake in a preheated oven at 325 degrees for one hour and 10 minutes. Test with toothpick to make sure cake is done. To make frosting, mix all ingredients together and beat until smooth. Frost cake.

Kids love it!

The Only Great Pound Cake

½ cup shortening
2 sticks butter (the real thing)
3 cups sugar
5 eggs
3½ cups flour
½ teaspoon baking powder
1 cup milk
1 teaspoon rum flavoring
1 teaspoon coconut flavoring

Glaze:

1 cup sugar
⅓ cup water
½ teaspoon almond extract

Preheat oven to 325 degrees. In mixer bowl, cream together shortening, butter and sugar. Add eggs; beat 4 minutes. Combine flour and baking powder and add dry ingredients and milk alternately to butter mixture, beginning and ending with flour. Add rum and coconut flavorings. Pour into a large greased and floured tube pan. Bake for 1 hour and 35 minutes. Test with toothpick for doneness. (Do not open door during baking.) Right before cake should be done, bring sugar and water to a rolling boil. Remove from heat and add almond extract. While cake is still in pan, pour the glaze over cake and let stand about 30 minutes before removing from pan.

Red Velvet Pound Cake

3 cups sugar
¾ cup shortening
6 eggs
1 teaspoon vanilla
¼ teaspoon salt
3 cups flour
1 cup milk
2 (1 ounce) bottles red food coloring

Icing:

1 (1 pound) box powdered sugar
1 (3 ounce) package cream cheese, softened
½ stick margarine, softened
3 tablespoons milk
Red sprinkles

Cream sugar and shortening together. Add eggs one at a time, beating after each addition. Add vanilla, mix. Add salt, flour and milk alternately beginning and ending with flour. Add food coloring; beat until smooth. Bake in a greased and floured tube pan at 325 degrees for 1 hour and 30 minutes or until cake tests done. Let cake rest in the pan for 10 minutes. Take cake out of pan and let cool completely. Frost. To make icing, cream together the powdered sugar, cream cheese, margarine and milk; mix well. Ice cake and top with a few red sprinkles over the white icing.

*So pretty and kids love it! The icing and color
make this an extra special pound cake.*

The Best Fresh Apple Cake

1½ cups oil
2 cups sugar
3 eggs
2½ cups sifted flour
½ teaspoon salt
1 teaspoon soda
2 teaspoons baking powder
½ teaspoon cinnamon
1 teaspoon vanilla
3 cups peeled and grated apples
1 cup chopped pecans

Glaze:
2 tablespoons margarine, melted
2 tablespoons milk
1 cup powdered sugar
1 teaspoon vanilla
¼ teaspoon lemon extract

Grease and flour tube pan. Mix oil, sugar and eggs and beat well. In a separate bowl, sift together flour, salt, soda, baking powder and cinnamon. Gradually add flour mixture to creamed mixture. Add vanilla and fold in apples and pecans and pour into tube pan. Bake at 350 degrees for 1 hour. After cake has cooled, invert onto serving plate. For the glaze, combine and mix all ingredients together and drizzle over cake.

Christmas Lemon Pecan Cake

1 (1.5 ounce) bottle lemon extract
4 cups pecan halves
4 sticks butter
3 cups sugar
3½ cups flour, divided
6 eggs
½ pound candied green pineapple, cut into smaller pieces
½ pound candied red cherries, cut in half
1½ teaspoons baking powder
½ cup flour

Pour lemon extract over pecans in a medium bowl; toss, then set aside. Grease and flour a tube cake pan. In a large mixing bowl, cream butter and sugar until fluffy. Sift 3 cups of the flour and baking powder together in a separate bowl. Add eggs to the butter-sugar mixture, one at a time, alternately with the flour mixture. With the pineapple and cherries cut, add the ½ cup flour and mix so that the fruit is well covered by the flour. Fold in fruit and pecans. Pour into the tube pan and bake at 275 degrees for 2½ to 2 hours and 45 minutes. Test after 2½ hours for doneness. Cool and remove carefully from pan.

This cake is delicious the day you make it and still better after several days! Try it and you will want it every Christmas!

Apple Date Pecan Cake

2 cups sugar
1½ cups oil
3 eggs
2 teaspoons vanilla
2½ cups flour
1 teaspoon soda
½ teaspoon salt
1½ teaspoons cinnamon
¼ teaspoon ground ginger
3 cups chopped apples
1 (8 ounce) package chopped dates
1 cup chopped pecans

Glaze:
1 cup sugar
1⅓ cup water
1 teaspoon almond extract

Blend together the sugar, oil, eggs and vanilla. Beat well. Add the flour, soda, salt, cinnamon and ginger; beating well. Fold in the apples, dates and pecans. Pour into a 10 inch greased and floured tube pan. Bake in a preheated oven at 325 degrees for 1 hour and 30 minutes or until cake tests done. Right before cake is done, bring sugar and water to a rolling boll. Remove from heat and add almond extract. Pour glaze over hot cake while still in pan. Let stand about 20 minutes before removing from pan.

Orange Date Cake

4 cups flour
1 teaspoon soda
2 sticks margarine, softened
2½ cups sugar
4 eggs
1½ cups buttermilk
1 teaspoon orange extract
1 tablespoon grated orange rind
1 (11 ounce) can mandarin oranges
1 (8 ounce) package pre-chopped dates
1 cup chopped pecans

Glaze:
½ cup orange juice
1¼ cups sugar
1 teaspoon orange rind
½ teaspoon orange extract

Sift flour and soda together. Set aside. Cream together the margarine and sugar. Add eggs, one at a time, beating well. Add buttermilk and dry ingredients alternately, ending with dry ingredients. Add orange extract and rind; beat well. Stir in oranges, dates and pecans. Pour into a greased and floured bundt pan and bake at 350 degrees for 1 hour and 15 minutes or until cake tests done. Remove from oven and pour glaze over cake while still in pan. To make glaze, mix orange juice, sugar, orange rind and extract. Bring to boiling point; then cool.

This is so moist and good – if you don't happen to have buttermilk on hand just put about 2 tablespoons of lemon juice in 1½ cups of milk and let it set 10 or 15 minutes presto, you'll have buttermilk.

Pumpkin Pie Pound Cake

1 cup Crisco
1¼ cups sugar
¾ cup packed brown sugar
5 eggs, room temperature
1 cup canned pumpkin
2½ cups flour
2 teaspoons cinnamon
1 teaspoon ground nutmeg
½ teaspoon mace
½ teaspoon salt
1 teaspoon baking soda
½ cup orange juice, room temperature
2 teaspoons vanilla
1½ cups chopped pecans

Icing:
2 cups powdered sugar
¾ stick margarine, melted
3 tablespoons orange juice
¼ teaspoon orange extract

Cream together the shortening and sugars for about 5 minutes. Add the eggs, one at a time, mixing well after each addition. Blend in the pumpkin. In a separate bowl, mix together the flour, spices, salt and baking soda, mixing well. Gradually beat the dry ingredients into batter until well mixed. Fold in the orange juice, vanilla and chopped pecans. Pour into a greased and floured bundt pan. Bake in a preheated oven at 325 degrees for one hour and 5 to 10 minutes, or until a tester comes out clean. Allow the cake to rest in the pan for 10 to 15 minutes, then turn cake out onto a rack to cool completely before icing. For the icing, thoroughly mix all icing ingredients together. Ice the cooled cake.

*How could you miss – having pumpkin pie and
pound cake all rolled up in one recipe!*

Amaretto Cake

1½ cups sliced almonds
1 box yellow cake mix
1 (3¾ ounce) box vanilla pudding mix
3 eggs
⅓ cup corn oil
¼ cup Amaretto
¾ cup orange juice
1 ½ teaspoon almond flavoring

Glaze:
4 tablespoons margarine
¾ cup sugar
¼ cup water
⅓ cup Amaretto

Preheat oven to 325 degrees. Spread almonds on a baking sheet and place in oven for 8 to 10 minutes or until golden brown. Remove and set aside. Grease and flour a bundt pan; sprinkle ½ cup almonds in bottom of pan. In mixing bowl, combine cake mix, pudding mix, eggs, oil, Amaretto, orange juice and almond flavoring. Mix and beat until fluffy. Fold in remaining almonds; pour into bundt pan and cook 1 hour at 325 degrees (test cake with toothpick for doneness). Invert on cake plate. For glaze: mix margarine, sugar and water in a saucepan. Bring to a boil; boil 2 minutes. Add Amaretto. Prick cake with toothpick and spoon glaze over cake.

Easy Favorite Cake

1 box Betty Crocker yellow cake mix
3 eggs
1¼ cups water
⅓ cup oil
1 box coconut pecan icing mix (this is a dry mix)

In mixer bowl, combine the cake mix, eggs, water and oil. Beat well. Stir in 1 box coconut pecan icing mix; mixing well. Pour into a greased and floured bundt pan. Bake in a preheated oven at 350 degrees for 45 minutes. Test with a toothpick.

All these ingredients you can always have on hand
to make hurriedly when you need to take food to
*friends in need. So good and so **easy.***

Easy Pineapple Cake

2 cups sugar
2 cups flour
1 (20 ounce) can crushed pineapple, undrained
1 teaspoon baking soda
½ teaspoon salt
1 teaspoon vanilla

Icing:

1 (8 ounce) package cream cheese, softened
1 stick margarine, melted
1 cup powdered sugar
1 cup chopped pecans

Mixing by hand, combine all cake ingredients. Mix well. Pour into a greased and floured 9 x 13 inch baking pan. Bake at 350 degrees for 30 to 35 minutes. Beat with mixer, the cream cheese, margarine and powdered sugar. Add the chopped pecans and pour over the hot cake.

Pina Colada Cake

1 (18 ounce) package orange cake mix
3 eggs
1¼ cups water
⅓ cup oil
1 can sweetened condensed milk
1 (15 ounce) can coconut cream
1 cup coconut
1 (8 ounce) can crushed pineapple, drained
1 (8 ounce) carton Cool Whip

In the mixing bowl, combine cake mix, eggs, water and oil. Beat 3 or 4 minutes and pour into a deep, greased and floured 10 x 14 inch baking pan. Bake at 350 degrees for 35 minutes. When cake is done, punch holes in cake with fork so frosting will soak into cake. Mix together sweetened condensed milk, coconut cream, coconut and pineapple. While cake is still warm pour mixture over top of the cake. Refrigerate; when cake is cold, spread a layer of Cool Whip over cake and return to refrigerator.

Rum Sugar Pound Cake

3 sticks butter, softened
1 (16 ounce) package brown sugar
1 cup sugar
5 large eggs
¾ cup milk
¼ cup rum
2 teaspoons vanilla
3 cups flour
2 teaspoons baking powder
¼ teaspoon salt
1½ cups chopped pecans

In the electric mixer, beat butter and sugars at medium speed about 5 minutes. Add eggs, one at a time, beating just until yellow disappears. Combine milk, rum and vanilla. Combine flour, baking powder and salt. Add half the flour mixture and mix. Add the milk mixture and mix. Add remaining flour mixture, beating at low speed. Fold in pecans. Pour into a greased and floured tube pan. Bake in a preheated 325 degree oven for 1 hour and 25 minutes. Test with a toothpick to make sure cake is done. Cool in pan for 20 minutes. Remove from pan; cool.

If you don't want to use the rum, just add another
¼ cup of milk and 2 teaspoons of rum flavoring.

Oreo Cake

1 (18½ ounce) package white cake mix
1¼ cups water
⅓ cup oil
4 egg whites
1 ¼ cups coarsely crushed Oreo cookies

Frosting:
4¼ cups powdered sugar
2 sticks butter, softened
1 cup shortening (not butter flavored)
1 teaspoon almond flavoring
½ cup crushed Oreo cookies
¼ cup chopped pecans

Grease and flour two 8 inch or 9 inch round cake pans. Preheat oven to 350 degrees. In a large mixer bowl, combine cake mix, water, oil and egg whites; blend on low speed until moistened. Then beat 2 minutes at highest speed. Gently fold in the coarsely crushed cookies. Pour batter into prepared pans. Bake for 25–30 minutes or until toothpick inserted in center comes out clean. Cool 10 minutes; then remove from pan. Let cool completely. For frosting, beat together, with mixer, all the ingredients in the frosting except crushed cookie pieces. Ice the first layer, place second layer on top and ice top and sides. Sprinkle the ¾ cup crushed Oreo cookies and the pecans on top.

My son always wanted "white cake" for his birthday, but since I found this recipe, he says "combine a white cake and Oreo cookies and you have the best of all cakes (of course he really likes all the creamy white icing)!

Praline Pear Cake

2½ cups flour
1½ cups sugar
1½ teaspoons baking soda
¼ teaspoon baking powder
1½ teaspoons ground cinnamon
½ teaspoon salt
½ teaspoon ground cloves
¼ teaspoon ground ginger
½ cup shortening
1 (29 ounce) can pear halves, drained and pureed
2 eggs
⅔ cup golden raisins

Praline Topping:

1⅓ cups packed brown sugar
1 stick margarine
⅓ cup half and half
¾ cup flaked coconut
1 cup chopped pecans

Grease and flour 9 x 13 inch baking pan. Mix flour, sugar, baking soda, baking powder, cinnamon, salt, cloves and ginger Add the shortening, pureed pears and eggs; beat on low speed 30 seconds, scraping bowl occasionally. Then beat on medium speed for 3 minutes. Fold in raisins and pour into prepared pan. Bake in a preheated 350 degree oven for 40 to 45 minutes. Test with a wooden pick inserted in center after 40 minutes to see if cake is done. While cake is baking, mix together the brown sugar, margarine and half and half in a medium saucepan. Bring to a boil while stirring constantly. Remove from burner and add the coconut and pecans to the topping. Spread over warm cake. Cut in squares. Serve at room temperature.

This cake is moist and delicious - and even better with a dab of whipped cream on top.

Coconut Pecan Cake

Cake:
2 cups flour
1½ cups sugar
Dash of salt
2 teaspoons soda
1 (20 ounce) can crushed pineapple, plus juice

Icing:
1½ cups sugar
1 (5 ounce) can evaporated milk
1 stick margarine
1 cup flaked coconut
1 cup chopped pecans
1 teaspoon vanilla
Dash of salt

Mix all of the cake ingredients together with a spoon and pour into a greased and floured 9 x 13 inch baking pan. Bake in a preheated oven for 35 minutes at 350 degrees. Leave in pan. For the icing, start just before cake is done and mix sugar, milk and margarine in a saucepan; boil 2 minutes. Add the coconut, pecans, vanilla and salt. Pour over the cake as soon as it comes out of the oven. When cake has cooled, cover with foil. When ready to serve, cut in squares. Serves 12.

Ranch Spice Cake

2½ cups flour
1 teaspoon baking powder
1 teaspoon cinnamon
½ teaspoon salt
½ teaspoon ginger
½ teaspoon allspice
½ teaspoon nutmeg
1 stick margarine, softened
½ cup sugar
1½ cups packed brown sugar
2 eggs
1 teaspoon vanilla
1 teaspoon baking soda
1¼ cups buttermilk

Caramel Icing:
1½ cups packed brown sugar
1 cup sugar
1 stick margarine
⅓ cup milk
1 egg
½ cup chopped pecans

Grease a 9 x 13 baking pan; set aside. Sift together first 7 ingredients. In a mixing bowl, beat margarine, sugars, eggs and vanilla until fluffy. Dissolve soda in buttermilk. Beat in half flour mixture; add buttermilk; beat. Add remaining flour; beat. Pour into prepared pan. Bake at 350 degrees for 45 minutes. Cool. For icing: in a saucepan, combine all ingredients except vanilla and pecans. Bring to a boil and boil stirring constantly for 4 minutes. Add pecans; pour over cake.

Nutty Cherry Cake

2 cups sugar
1 stick margarine, softened
2 eggs
2½ cups flour
2 teaspoons soda
1 (16 ounce) can bing cherries, drained
1 cup chopped pecans

Cherry sauce:
1 (16 ounce) can cherry pie filling
⅓ cup sugar
⅓ cup water

Preheat oven to 350 degrees. In mixing bowl, combine sugar, margarine and eggs; beat several minutes. Add flour and soda, mix well. Fold in cherries and pecans. Pour into a greased and floured 9 x 13 inch baking pan. Bake 35 minutes. Test with toothpick for doneness. For sauce, combine cherry pie filling, sugar and water. Heat to dissolve sugar, but not to boiling stage. When ready to serve, pour about ⅓ cup of hot sauce over a square of cake. Good at room temperature too.

Almond Joy Cake

1 German chocolate cake mix
1½ cups water
⅓ cup oil
3 eggs
¾ cup evaporated milk
1 cup sugar
24 large marshmallows
1 (3½ ounce) can coconut
½ cup evaporated milk
½ stick margarine
1 (12 ounce) package milk chocolate chips
1 cup toasted almond slivers*

Grease and flour a large 10½ x 15½ inch baking pan. Preheat oven to 350 degrees. In mixing bowl, combine cake mix, water, oil and eggs. Beat 4 or 5 minutes. Pour into baking pan and bake 30 to 35 minutes (test with toothpick). While cake is still hot, combine in a saucepan, the ¾ cup evaporated milk, sugar and marshmallows. Bring to a boil, lower heat, simmer while stirring until marshmallows are melted. Add coconut and pour over hot cake. Punch holes in cake with a toothpick so mixture will soak into cake. Cool. Using the same saucepan (no need to wash), combine ½ cup evaporated milk, margarine and milk chocolate chips. Heat, while stirring, until chocolate chips are melted. Add almonds. Pour over cooled cake.

*To toast almond slivers, place in shallow pan and toast in a 275 degree oven for about 10 to 15 minutes.

Coconut Cake Deluxe

1 package yellow cake mix
Ingredients called for in cake mix
1 can sweetened condensed milk
1 can coconut cream
1 can coconut
1 (8 ounce) carton Cool Whip

Mix yellow cake according to package directions. Pour into a greased and floured 9 x 13 baking pan. Bake at 350 degrees for 30 to 35 minutes or until toothpick inserted in center comes out clean. While cake is warm, punch holes in cake about two inches apart. Pour sweetened condensed milk over cake and spread around until all milk has soaked into cake. Then pour the can of coconut cream over cake and sprinkle the coconut on top. Let cool and frost with Cool Whip. Serves 12-15.

This cake is really moist and delicious and can be
frozen if you need to make ahead of time.

Strawberry Fluff Explosion

2 sticks margarine, softened
½ cup packed brown sugar
2 cups flour
1½ cups chopped pecans
2 egg whites
1 tablespoon lemon juice
1 cup sugar
2 (10 ounce) packages sweetened strawberries, thawed
1 tablespoon vanilla
1 (12 ounce) carton Cool Whip

Combine and mix together the margarine, brown sugar and flour until crumbly. Add pecans and spread on a cookie sheet. Bake at 350 degrees about 15 minutes. Spread this crumbly mixture in a large 10 x 14 inch glass casserole dish. Cool. In mixer bowl, beat the egg whites for 5 minutes, then add the lemon juice, 1 cup sugar and both packages of strawberries and beat another 15 minutes. This mixture will grow and grow and grow! Fold in the Cool Whip and pour over the crumbly crust mixture. Freeze.

This is one of the lightest, fluffiest, most delicious desserts you will ever eat! I talked a good friend out of this recipe.

Be ready. This explodes slowly, but surely. Have a big bowl. You'll never forget it. It's a real blast.

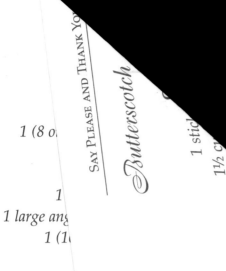

Butterscotch

1 (8 o

1 stic

1½ c

1

1 large an

1 (1

Add sugar and mil
in coconut and pec
pieces. Spread in a l
hours. Add pie filli
mixture. It will not c   .... in
clumps, making a p   ......ite dessert. Refrigerate.
Serves 15 to 16.

My Mother named this after me. — S.J.
This gets rave reviews whenever I serve it. It's one of my favorites.

Oreo Sunday

EASY

1 stick margarine
1 (19-ounce) package Oreos, crushed
½ gallon vanilla ice cream, softened
2 jars fudge sauce
1 (12-ounce) carton Cool Whip
Maraschino cherries

Melt margarine in a 9 x 13 inch pan. Reserve about ½ cup crushed Oreos for top and mix remaining with margarine to form a crust in pan (press into pan). Spread softened ice cream over crust; and add layer of fudge sauce. Top with carton of Cool Whip. Sprinkle with remaining crumbs. Garnish with cherries. Freeze until ready to serve. Serves 12.

Heaven

Crust:
margarine, melted
ps graham cracker crumbs
⅓ cup packed brown sugar

First and third layers:
1 (8 ounce) cream cheese, softened
1 can sweetened condensed milk
½ teaspoon almond extract
1 (12 ounce) container Cool Whip

Second layer:
1 stick margarine
2 (2 ounce) packages sliced almonds
1 cup coconut
1 (8 ounce) jar butterscotch topping
¾ cup graham cracker crumbs

Topping:
1 (8 ounce) jar butterscotch topping

In a mixing bowl, mix together all crust ingredients together. Pat into a greased 9 x 13 inch baking pan. Bake at 350 degrees for 12 to 14 minutes or until it is lightly browned. For first layer: in mixing bowl, cream together cream cheese, condensed milk and almond extract until smooth. Fold in Cool Whip. Pour ½ of this mixture onto cooled crust. Chill in freezer for about 30 minutes. For second layer: melt margarine in a saucepan; add almonds, coconut, butterscotch topping and graham crackers. Mix. Sprinkle over cream cheese layer. For third layer: pour remaining cream cheese mixture over almond-butterscotch layer. Freeze. When frozen, pour remaining jar of butterscotch ~er top and swirl. Return to freezer. Take out of freezer 5 or 10 ·tes before serving.

Butterscotch lovers rejoice!

Strawberry Pineapple ⌁

1¼ cups flour
⅓ cup packed brown sugar
1 stick margarine, softened
½ cup chopped pecans

First layer:
¾ cup sugar
3 tablespoons cornstarch
1 (15 ½ ounce) can crushed pineapple, undrained

Second layer:
1 (8 ounce) package cream cheese, softened
1½ cups powdered sugar
1 (8 ounce) carton Cool Whip

Third layer:
½ cup sugar
3 tablespoons cornstarch
2 (10 ounce) packages frozen sweetened strawberries

Topping:
1 cup heavy cream
⅓ cup powdered sugar

In a mixing bowl, combine and mix flour, sugar and margarine. Beat until crumbly. Add pecans. Pat into a greased 9 x 13 inch baking pan. Bake at 350 degrees for about 13 to 14 minutes. Cool. First layer: in a saucepan, combine sugar and cornstarch. Add pineapple and cook on medium heat until thickened. Pour over crumb crust. Place in freezer until next layer is ready. Second layer: in mixing bowl, beat together cream cheese and powdered sugar; fold in Cool Whip. Pour over the pineapple layer. Freeze about 30 minutes. Third layer: mix sugar and cornstarch in a saucepan. Add strawberries and cook on medium heat until thick. Pour over cream cheese layer. Freeze. Whip heavy cream; add sugar and mix. Cover top with whipped cream. Remove from freezer 15 minutes before serving.

Cream Cake

Fiesta

...o 40 lady fingers

First layer:
vanilla ice cream, softened
...an frozen orange juice, undiluted

Second layer:
4 tablespoons cornstarch
1½ cups sugar
1 (8 ounce) can crushed pineapple, undrained
1 (12 ounce) package frozen raspberries, thawed

Third layer:
3 cups vanilla ice cream, softened
1 teaspoon almond extract
1 teaspoon rum extract
10 maraschino cherries, chopped
½ cup chopped pecans

Line lady fingers around a 9 inch springform pan. Place lady fingers on bottom of pan. In a mixing bowl, mix softened ice cream and orange juice concentrate. Mix and pour over lady fingers. Place in freezer until next layer is ready. For second layer: in a saucepan, mix cornstarch and sugar. Add pineapple; stir. On medium heat, cook, stirring constantly, until thickened. Add raspberries and mix. Cool and pour over first layer. Freeze 5 or 6 hours before putting on third layer. For third layer: mix all ingredients together and pour over second layer. Freeze several hours before slicing. Serves 16.

Lemon Lush

1¼ cups flour
⅔ cup margarine
½ cup chopped pecans
1 cup powdered sugar
1 (8 ounce) package cream cheese, softened
1 (12 ounce) carton Cool Whip, divided
2 (3¾ ounces each) packages instant lemon pudding
1 tablespoon lemon juice
2¾ cups milk

Mix flour, margarine and pecans. Pat into a 9 x 13 baking dish and bake 15 minutes at 375 degrees. Beat together powdered sugar and cream cheese until fluffy and fold in 2 cups of the Cool Whip. Spread on nut crust. Mix pudding, lemon juice and milk and beat. Spread over the second layer. Top with remaining Cool Whip and refrigerate. To serve, cut into squares.

Ice Box Dessert

1 pound vanilla wafers, crushed to make crumbs
½ stick margarine, melted
1¾ cups milk
1 pound marshmallows
1 cup whipping cream, whipped
1 (15½ ounce) can crushed pineapple, drained

Mix together the vanilla wafers and margarine. Pour ¾ of the vanilla wafers into a greased 9 x 13 inch dish. Pat down to make crust. In a medium saucepan, scald milk (do not bring to boiling point) and add marshmallows; keep on low heat while stirring until marshmallows are melted. Cool to room temperature. Fold in whipped cream and pineapple. Pour over crust. Sprinkle with remaining vanilla wafer crumbs. Refrigerate. To serve, cut in squares. Serves 12.

Orange Bavarian Cream

1½ cups vanilla wafer crumbs (about 34 wafers)
2 (6 ounce) cartons orange yogurt
1 (3½ ounce) package vanilla instant pudding mix
¼ cup powdered sugar
1 (8 ounce) carton Cool Whip
½ teaspoon orange flavoring
3 (11 ounce) cans mandarin oranges, drained

Crush vanilla wafers in food processor or crush in a baggie. In mixing bowl, beat yogurt and pudding mix (dry) together for about 30 seconds. Fold in powdered sugar, Cool Whip and orange flavoring. Layer in 8 parfait glasses with oranges and crushed vanilla wafers. Save enough to top with a teaspoon or so of crumbs and one orange slice.

EASY Creamy Banana Pudding

1 can sweetened condensed milk
1½ cups cold water
1 (3¾ ounce) package instant vanilla pudding mix
1 (8 ounce) carton Cool Whip
36 vanilla wafers
3 bananas

In a large bowl, combine sweetened condensed milk and water. Add pudding mix and beat well. Chill 5 minutes. Fold in Cool Whip. Spoon 1 cup pudding mixture into a 3 quart glass serving bowl. Top with the wafers, bananas and pudding. Repeat layering twice, ending with pudding. Cover and chill. Keep refrigerated.

Quick and easy!

Fruit Sundae

1 (12 ounce) box vanilla wafers
1 stick margarine, melted
¾ cup milk
1 (16 ounce) package marshmallows
2 (8 ounce) cartons Cool Whip
1 (16 ounce) frozen sweetened strawberries, thawed
1 (16 ounce) can crushed pineapple
1 (3½ ounce) coconut
1 cup chopped pecans

Crush vanilla wafers in food processor or you can crush wafers in a large baggie with a rolling pin. Place crushed vanilla wafers in a Pam sprayed 9 x 13 inch baking dish. Pour melted margarine over vanilla wafers and mix well. Remove about ¾ cup of the crumbs and set aside. Pack crumbs in dish and refrigerate. Combine milk and marshmallows in a large saucepan. Place over low heat, stirring constantly until marshmallows melt. Cool. Fold 1 carton of the Cool Whip into marshmallow mixture and pour over crushed vanilla wafers. Chill. Drain strawberries and pineapple. In a medium mixing bowl, combine strawberries, pineapple, coconut and pecans; toss. Spread over chilled marshmallow mixture. Cover with second carton of Cool Whip. Sprinkle ¾ cup of reserved crumbs over Cool Whip. Refrigerate overnight.

Call Jennie Craig or
Weight Watchers. — BCJ

Pecan Bread Pudding with Bourbon Sauce

3 eggs

1½ cups sugar

2 tablespoons brown sugar

½ teaspoon nutmeg

2¾ cups whipping cream

¼ cup butter, melted

½ cup pecans

½ cup raisins

4 cups Texas Toast (crust removed and cubed)

Bourbon Sauce:

½ cup sugar

3 tablespoons brown sugar

1 tablespoon flour

1 egg

2 tablespoons butter, melted

1¼ cups whipping cream

¼ cup bourbon

Combine the 3 eggs, sugars, nutmeg, whipping cream, butter, pecans and raisins. Place bread in a 6 x 10 loaf pan and pour the egg, sugar, whipping cream mixture over the bread. Bake, covered, at 375 degrees for 20 minutes then remove the covering and cook another 30 minutes. Cool. For the sauce, whisk together in a heavy pan, the sugars, flour, egg, butter and whipping cream. Over a medium heat, cook, stirring constantly, until mixture has thickened. Add bourbon to sauce and mix well. To serve, slice the Bread Pudding and serve with 2 or 3 tablespoons of the Bourbon Sauce. Serves 8.

Really delicious!

Caramel Apple Mousse

1½ sticks margarine
⅔ cup sugar
2½ teaspoons lemon juice
¼ cup water
½ teaspoon cinnamon
2 tablespoons rum
5 or 6 medium apples, peeled and thinly sliced
½ pint whipping cream, whipped
¼ cup sugar
1 teaspoon vanilla
Peanut brittle, slightly crushed

Melt margarine in large skillet and add sugar, juice and water. Continue cooking until sugar is dissolved and syrup is slightly thickened and golden in color (about 10 minutes). Remove from heat and add cinnamon, rum and apples. Cook apples in syrup until thoroughly coated and softened (about 3 to 4 minutes). Remove apples from syrup. Cool. Add sugar to whipped cream and fold apples into whipped cream. Spoon into parfait glasses or crystal sherberts and chill several hours. Just before serving sprinkle generously with crushed peanut brittle.

Toffee Cream Surprise

1 cup buttermilk
1 (3 ounce) package French vanilla instant pudding
1 (12 ounce) carton Cool Whip
1 (12 ounce) package Keebler's toffee toppers,
fudge covered, shortbread cookies
1 (10 ounce) jar maraschino cherries, drained, halved
1 cup chopped pecans
1 cup miniature marshmallows

In a mixing bowl, combine buttermilk and vanilla pudding. Beat with a whisk until thoroughly mixed. Fold in Cool Whip. Lightly crumble cookies with the knife blade of food processor. Don't pulverize cookies; you may have to break a few cookies up by hand. Leave some cookies in chunks. Fold cookies, cherries, pecans and marshmallows into pudding mixture. Refrigerate in covered bowl and serve in individual sherbets. Best served same day. Serves 12.

Christmas Cookies

2 sticks margarine, softened
¾ cup sugar
1 cup packed brown sugar
1 teaspoon vanilla
2 eggs
2½ cups flour
1 teaspoon baking soda
½ teaspoon salt
1 (12 ounce) package white chocolate chips
I cup chopped pecans
1 (3½ ounce) can coconut
20 red candied cherries, chopped
20 green candied cherries, chopped

In a mixing bowl, cream together the margarine, sugars, vanilla and eggs. Beat well. Add flour, baking soda and salt. Mix well. Stir in chocolate chips, pecans, coconut and cherries. Drop dough by teaspoon onto an ungreased cookie sheet. Bake in a preheated 350 degree oven for 8 to 10 minutes. Cool before storing.

We'll see. — BCJ

309

Whippersnappers

¾ cup packed brown sugar
¾ cup white sugar
1½ cups shortening
2 large eggs
1½ cups flour
½ teaspoon baking soda
½ teaspoon salt
2¾ cups oats
½ cup chopped pecans
½ cup peanut butter
1½ teaspoons vanilla
1 (6 ounce) package chocolate chips

Cream together sugars and shortening. Add eggs and beat. Sift together flour, soda and salt. Add to creamed mixture. Stir in oats, pecans, peanut butter, vanilla and chocolate chips. Drop by teaspoon on a cookie sheet. Bake at 350 degrees for 12 to 14 minutes or until cookies begin to brown on the edge.

Party Kisses

3 egg whites
1 cup sugar
2 teaspoons vanilla
½ teaspoon almond extract
3⅓ cups Frosted Flakes
1 cup chopped pecans

In a mixing bowl, beat egg whites until stiff. Gradually add sugar and extracts. Fold in Frosted Flakes and pecans. Drop by teaspoonfuls on a cookie sheet lined with waxed paper. Bake at 250 degrees for 40 minutes. Makes 4 dozen.

Orange Fingers

3¼ cups vanilla wafer crumbs
1 (16 ounce) box powdered sugar
2 cups chopped pecans
1 (16 ounce) can frozen orange juice concentrate, thawed
1 stick margarine, melted
1 cup flaked coconut

Mix vanilla wafer crumbs, powdered sugar and pecans together. Stir in orange juice and margarine. Shape into 2 inch fingers and roll in coconut. Refrigerate.

Baylor Cookies

1 cup shortening
¼ cup packed brown sugar
1 cup sugar
1 egg
¼ teaspoon salt
1½ teaspoons vanilla
2 cups flour
2 teaspoons baking powder
1 cup chopped pecans

Combine shortening, sugars, egg, salt and vanilla and mix well. Add flour and baking powder and mix until well blended. Add pecans and mix. Divide dough in half and roll out in a long jelly roll shape, on a sheet of floured wax paper. Place rolled dough on another piece of wax paper and roll up in paper. Refrigerate for several hours. When dough is thoroughly chilled, slice in ¼ inch slices. Bake on cookie sheet at 350 degrees for about 15 minutes or until just slightly browned.

My grandmother made these at Allen Hall when my Dad went to Baylor University. I grew up on these and they're the greatest. —S.J.

Sierra Nuggets

2 sticks margarine
1 cup packed brown sugar
1½ cups white sugar
1 tablespoon milk
2 teaspoons vanilla
2 eggs
I cup crushed flake cereal
3 cups oatmeal
1½ cups flour
1¼ teaspoons baking soda
1 teaspoon salt
2 teaspoons cinnamon
¼ teaspoon nutmeg
⅛ teaspoon clove
½ cup coconut
2 cups chocolate chips
1 cup walnuts or pecans

In a large mixing bowl, cream together the margarine and sugars and beat in milk, vanilla and eggs. Then stir in flake cereal and oatmeal. Sift together the flour, baking soda, salt and seasonings. Gradually add to cookie mixture. Stir in coconut, chocolate chips and nuts. Drop by teaspoon on cookie sheet and bake at 350 degrees for 10 to 15 minutes.

Peanut Krispies

1 stick margarine
2 cups peanut butter
1 (16 ounce) box powdered sugar
3½ cups Rice Krispies
¾ cup peanuts, chopped

In a large saucepan, melt margarine. Add peanut butter and powdered sugar; mix well. Add Rice Krispies and peanuts. Mix. Drop by teaspoonfuls onto wax paper.

Snappy Treats

EASY

3 cups quick rolled oats
1 cup chocolate chips
½ cup coconut
½ cup chopped pecans
2 cups sugar
1½ sticks margarine
½ cup evaporated milk

Mix oats, chocolate chips, coconut and pecans in a large bowl. Bring sugar, margarine and milk to a rapid boil and boil 1½ minutes, stirring constantly. Pour hot mixture over mixture in bowl and stir until chocolate chips melt. Drop by teaspoon on waxed paper. Cool at room temperature. Store in covered container. (If you use white chocolate chips, it makes this real colorful if you add ¾ cup candied cherries, cut up.)

Seven Layer Cookies

1 stick margarine
1 cup crushed graham crackers
1 (6 ounce) package semisweet chocolate bits
1 (6 ounce) package butterscotch bits
1 (3½ ounce) can coconut
1 can sweetened condensed milk
1 cup chopped pecans

Melt margarine in a 9 x 13 inch baking pan. Sprinkle other ingredients on top in order as they are listed. Do not stir or mix. Bake at 350 degrees for 30 minutes. Allow to cool before cutting.

Crunchy Cashew Cookies

2 sticks margarine, softened
1 cup sugar
¾ cup packed brown sugar
1 egg
2¼ cups flour
½ teaspoon soda
½ teaspoon cream of tartar
2 teaspoons vanilla
1 teaspoon almond extract
1½ cups chopped cashews

In a mixer bowl, cream margarine with the sugars; add egg. Beat. Blend in flour, soda and cream of tartar. Add vanilla, almond extract and cashews; mix thoroughly. Drop by teaspoonfuls onto a greased cookie sheet. Bake at 350 degrees for 10 to 12 minutes or until golden brown.

Chinese Cookies

1 (6 ounce) package chocolate chips
1 (6 ounce) package butterscotch chips
1 cup salted peanuts
1 can chow mein noodles

In a large saucepan, melt the chocolate and butterscotch chips. Add the peanuts and noodles. Mix well; drop by teaspoon on wax paper. Refrigerate just to harden.

All-Kids Peanut Butter Cookies

1 stick margarine, softened
¼ cup shortening
⅔ cup sugar
1 cup packed brown sugar
1 egg
1 cup crunchy peanut butter
1¾ cups flour
½ teaspoon baking powder
¾ teaspoon soda
¼ teaspoon salt

In mixing bowl, cream together the margarine, shortening sugars and egg; beating well. Add peanut butter and mix. Add all dry ingredients and mix well. Using a small size cookie scoop, place cookies onto an ungreased cookie sheet. Use a fork to flatten cookies. Criss-cross fork twice. Bake in a preheated 350 degree oven for about 12 minutes. Store covered.

This will make about 22 cookies so if you have a bunch of kids, you had better double this recipe. This was my son's favorite cookie when be was growing up.

305

Fudge Krispies

1 (12 ounce) package milk chocolate chips
¾ stick margarine
½ cup light corn syrup
1 teaspoon vanilla
¾ cup peanut butter
1 cup powdered sugar
4 cups Rice Krispies
½ cup chopped pecans

In a large saucepan, combine chips, margarine and corn syrup. Stir over low heat until melted. Add vanilla, peanut butter and powdered sugar. Mix well. Stir in cereal and pecans; mix well. Spread into a buttered 9 x 13 inch pan. Cut into squares.

White Chocolate and Almond Cookies

¾ cup firmly packed light brown sugar
½ cup sugar
1 stick margarine, softened
½ cup shortening
1½ teaspoons vanilla
1 egg
1¾ cups flour, plus 2 tablespoons
1 teaspoon baking soda
½ teaspoon salt
8 ounces white chocolate morsels
⅓ cup slivered almonds

In a large bowl, combine sugars, margarine, shortening, vanilla and egg. Blend well. Stir in flour, soda and salt. Blend well. Stir in white chocolate morsels and almonds. Mix well. Batter will

(Continued on Next Page)

(Continued)

be stiff. Drop by rounded teaspoonfuls onto an ungreased baking sheet. Bake in a 350 degree oven for about 10 minutes. They should be light golden brown. Store in container with a lid.

Favorite Chocolate Chip Cookies

1 stick margarine, softened
¾ cup sugar
¾ cup packed brown sugar
1 egg
1 tablespoon water
½ teaspoon vanilla
1 cup flour
½ teaspoon baking soda
1½ cups quick cooking oats
1 (6 ounce) package chocolate chips
½ cup chopped pecans

Preheat oven to 350 degrees. In a mixing bowl, combine margarine, sugars, egg, water and vanilla; beat. Add dry ingredients; mix well. Add oats, chocolate chips and pecans. Mix well. Drop by teaspoonfuls onto a cookie sheet and bake for about 12 to 15 minutes or until lightly browned.

Bosom your cards. — BCJ

Choc-O-Cherry Cookies

1 stick margarine, softened
1 cup sugar
1 egg
½ teaspoon vanilla
1½ cups flour
½ cup cocoa
¼ teaspoon salt
¼ teaspoon baking powder
¼ teaspoon baking soda
1 (10 ounce) jar maraschino cherries, well drained
1 (6 ounce) package chocolate chips

Cream margarine, sugar, egg and vanilla until light and fluffy. Add dry ingredients and mix. Cut cherries in fourths and add cherries and chocolate chips; mix. Drop by teaspoon on a cookie sheet and bake at 350 degrees for 15 minutes.

A chocolate lover's delight!

Mincemeat Cookies

2 sticks margarine, softened
1⅔ cups sugar
3 eggs, beaten
1 teaspoon soda
2 teaspoons hot water
½ teaspoon salt
3¼ cups flour
1¼ cups chopped pecans
1 cup prepared mincemeat

Grease cookie sheets. Cream margarine and add sugar

(Continued on Next Page)

318

(Continued)

gradually. Add eggs and then soda dissolved in water. Mix, add salt and the flour to creamed mixture. Mix well. Add pecans and mincemeat. Drop by teaspoon on cookie sheets. Bake at 350 degrees for 14 to 15 minutes or until cookies begin to brown.

For you "baby boomers" who don't know how good mincemeat is, don't overlook this recipe – it's great!

Macadamia Nut Cookies

½ cup shortening
1 stick margarine, softened
2½ cups flour
1 cup packed brown sugar
½ cup sugar
2 eggs
1 teaspoon vanilla
½ teaspoon butter flavoring
½ teaspoon baking soda
2 cups white chocolate chips
1 (3½ ounce) jar Macadamia nuts, chopped

In mixing bowl, beat shortening and margarine. Add half of flour and mix well. Add brown sugar, sugar, eggs, vanilla, butter flavoring and baking soda. Beat until mixture is well combined. Add remaining flour. Mix well and stir in chocolate pieces and nuts. Drop dough by teaspoon onto ungreased cookie sheet. Bake at 350 degrees for about 8 minutes.

Just like those good cookies you buy at the mall.

Date and Rice Krispy Cookies

1 cup sugar
½ stick margarine
2 eggs
1 package dates, cut up
3 cups Rice Krispies
1 cup very finely chopped pecans*

In a large saucepan, combine sugar, margarine, eggs and dates. Bring to a boil, reduce heat and cook 5 minutes, stirring constantly. Then add Rice Krispies and mix well. Rub shortening on hands and with a heaping tablespoon of cookie dough, form into balls and roll in chopped pecans. *Coconut could be used instead of pecans.

Pecan Squares

2 cups flour
½ cup powdered sugar
2 sticks margarine, cut up
1 (14 ounce) can sweetened condensed milk
2 eggs
1 teaspoon vanilla
1 (7.5 ounce) package Bits 0'Brickle chips
1 cup chopped pecans

Combine flour and powdered sugar in a medium bowl. Cut in margarine with a pastry blender or fork until crumbly. Press mixture evenly into a greased 9 x 13 inch baking pan. Bake at 350 degrees for 15 minutes. Combine sweetened condensed milk and next 4 ingredients. Pour over prepared crust. Bake at 350 degrees for 25 minutes or until golden. Cool and cut into squares. Makes 4 dozen.

Easy Blonde Brownies

1 pound box light brown sugar
4 eggs
2 cups biscuit mix
2 cups chopped pecans

In mixer, beat together the brown sugar, eggs and biscuit mix. Stir in the pecans and pour into a greased 9 x 13 inch baking pan. Bake in a preheated 350 degree oven for 35 minutes. Cool and cut into squares.

*This is another one of those recipes that seems too **easy** to be a recipe – and you already have everything right in the pantry. These brownies are so good and chewy!*

Lemon Angel Bars

1 (1 pound) package one-step angel food cake mix
1 (21 ounce) can lemon pie filling
1/3 cup margarine, softened
2 cups powdered sugar
2 tablespoons lemon juice

Combine the cake mix and lemon pie filling in a bowl and stir until well mixed. Pour into oiled and floured 9 x 13 inch baking pan. Bake at 350 degrees for 20 to 25 minutes (test with toothpick in center of cake for doneness). Just before cake is done, mix the margarine, powdered sugar and lemon juice together and spread over the hot layer. The cake will sink down a little in the middle, so with your spoon, make sure the icing is on the edges of cake as well as in the middle. When cool, cut into 18 to 24 bars. Store in refrigerator, but can be served room temperature or cold.

*This is one of those "crazy" recipes that you wonder if something so simple will work! But it does – **easy** and delicious lemon bars.*

Lemon Crumb Squares

1¼ sticks margarine, softened
½ cup sugar
½ cup packed brown sugar
1½ cups flour
1 teaspoon baking powder
½ teaspoon salt
1 cup quick-cooking oatmeal
1 can sweetened condensed milk
½ cup lemon juice

Cream margarine and sugars together in mixing bowl. Add dry ingredients and oatmeal; beat until the mixture is crumbly. Spread half the mixture in a 9 x 13 inch greased and floured baking pan and pat down. Set remaining mixture aside. In a separate bowl mix thoroughly sweetened condensed milk and lemon juice. Pour over crumbs in baking dish; then cover with the remaining crumbs. Bake at 350 degrees for 25 minutes. Cool at room temperature and cut into squares. Refrigerate.

Lemon Bars

2 sticks margarine
2 cups flour
½ cup powdered sugar
2 cups sugar
6 tablespoons flour
4 eggs, lightly beaten
6 tablespoons lemon juice
½ teaspoon lemon rind
Powdered sugar

Melt margarine in a 9 x 13 inch baking pan in oven. Add flour
(Continued on Next Page)

(Continued)

and powdered sugar and stir into melted margarine in pan. Mix well. Press down evenly and firmly and bake at 350 degrees for 15 minutes. For the filling, combine, in a mixing bowl the 2 cups sugar and 6 tablespoons flour; add eggs, lemon juice and lemon rind. Mix and pour over crust. Bake at 350 degrees for 20 minutes more. Cool and dust with powdered sugar. To serve, cut into squares.

Chewy Caramel Brownies

50 paper wrapped caramels (about 14 ounces)
1 (5 ounce) can evaporated milk, divided
1 box German chocolate cake mix
1½ sticks margarine, melted
1 cup chopped pecans
1 cup semi-sweet chocolate chips

In a pan over LOW heat, melt caramels, stirring constantly, with ⅓ cup of the evaporated milk. In mixer bowl combine cake mix with melted margarine and remaining milk. Spread one-half of the cake mixture into bottom of a greased 9 x 13 inch baking pan. Bake in a preheated 350 degree oven for 7 minutes. Sprinkle with pecans and chocolate chips. Spoon on melted caramels. Drop spoonfuls of the remaining cake mixture over top and lightly spread with the back of a spoon. Bake at 350 degrees for about 18 to 20 minutes. Cool completely before cutting into squares. Yield about 24 brownies. This is worth all the time it takes to unwrap those 50 caramels!

Buttery Walnut Squares

2 sticks butter, softened
1¾ cup packed brown sugar
1¾ cup flour

Topping:

1 cup packed brown sugar
4 eggs, lightly beaten
2 tablespoons flour
2 cups chopped walnuts
1 cup flaked coconut

For the crust, cream butter (please use the real thing) and sugar. Add flour and mix well. Pat mixture evenly in a greased 9 x 13 inch glass pan. Bake at 350 degrees for 15 minutes. For topping, in a medium-size bowl, combine sugar and eggs. Add flour and mix well. Fold in walnuts and coconut. Pour over crust. Bake at 350 degrees for 20 to 25 minutes or just until set in center. Cool in pan and cut into squares.

A scoop of ice cream really makes it good for a dessert.

Macadamia Bars

Crust:
2 sticks margarine, softened
2/3 cup sugar
2 cups flour

Filling:
4 eggs
1 cup flaked coconut
3 cups packed light brown sugar
2 (3.2 ounce) jars macadamia nuts, chopped
4 tablespoons flour
3 teaspoons vanilla extract
1 teaspoon baking powder

In a mixer bowl, cream together all crust ingredients. Press into a greased 9 x 13 inch baking dish. Bake in a 350 degree preheated oven for 20 minutes. In a medium bowl, lightly beat eggs and add remaining filling ingredients. Pour over hot baked crust and bake at 350 degrees for an additional 25 to 30 minutes. Cool completely and cut into small squares or you can cut in a larger square and serve with a dip of ice cream.

You could substitute 1½ cups pecans for the macadamia nuts.
Either way, they are moist, chewy and absolutely sinful.
Since I am from an area where pecans are plentiful, I like the
macadamia nuts — sounds more exotic!

SAY PLEASE AND THANK YOU

Iced Pineapple Squares

1½ cups sugar
2 cups flour
1½ teaspoons soda
½ teaspoon salt
1 (16 ounce) can crushed pineapple, undrained
2 eggs

Icing:

1½ cups sugar
1 stick margarine
1 (5 ounce) can evaporated milk
1 cup chopped pecans
1 (3½ ounce) can coconut
1 teaspoon vanilla

Preheat oven to 350 degrees. In mixer bowl, combine sugar, flour, soda, salt, pineapple and eggs; beat well. Pour into a 9 x 13 inch greased and floured pan. Bake for 35 minutes. Start cooking icing as the squares are baking. Mix sugar, margarine and evaporated milk together in a saucepan and boil 4 minutes, stirring constantly. Remove from heat and add the pecans, coconut and vanilla. Spread over hot squares. Serves 12.

Apricot Almond Bars

1 package yellow cake mix
1 stick margarine, melted
¾ cup finely chopped almonds
1 (12 ounce) jar apricot preserves (divided), slightly heated
1 (8 ounce) package cream cheese, softened
¼ cup sugar
2 tablespoons flour
⅛ teaspoon salt
1 egg
1 teaspoon vanilla
⅔ cup flaked coconut

In a large bowl, combine cake mix and margarine; mix by hand just until crumbly. Stir in almonds and reserve 1 cup crumb mixture. Lightly press remaining crumb mixture into a greased 9 x 13 inch baking pan. Carefully spread 1 cup of the preserves over crumb mixture, leaving a ¼ inch border. Beat cream cheese in mixer until smooth; add remaining preserves, sugar, flour, salt, egg, and vanilla; beating well. Carefully spread cream cheese mixture over top of preserves. Combine the 1 cup reserved crumb mixture and the coconut; mixing well. Sprinkle over cream cheese mixture. Bake at 350 degrees for 35 minutes or until center is set. Cool. Store in refrigerator.

You can do anything.
You just can't do everything. — BCJ

327

Coconut Cherry Squares

Pastry:

1⅓ cups flour
1¼ sticks margarine, softened
1½ cups powdered sugar

Filling:

3 eggs, beaten
1½ cups sugar
¾ cup flour
½ teaspoon salt
¾ teaspoon baking powder
1 teaspoon vanilla
¾ cup chopped pecans
¾ cup coconut
¾ cup maraschino cherries, drained and chopped

In mixer bowl, combine pastry ingredients and press into bottom of a 9 x 13 inch baking pan. Bake at 350 degrees for 20 minutes or just until golden. Set aside. Using the same mixer bowl, combine filling ingredients; mixing well. Spread over crust. Bake 25 minutes or until golden brown. Cool and cut into squares. You could give this an even more holiday look by using half green and half red maraschino cherries.

This is not only pretty- it's — good, good, good!

Almond Coconut Squares

2 cups graham cracker crumbs
3 tablespoons brown sugar
1 stick margarine, melted
1 (14 ounce) can sweetened condensed milk
1 (7 ounce) package coconut
I teaspoon vanilla

Topping:

1 (6 ounce) package chocolate chips
1 (6 ounce) package butterscotch chips
4 tablespoons margarine
6 tablespoons chunky peanut butter
½ cup slivered almonds

Mix graham cracker crumbs, brown sugar and margarine. Pat into a greased 9 x 13 inch baking pan. Bake in a preheated 325 degrees oven for 10 minutes. Cool. Combine sweetened condensed milk, coconut and vanilla. Pour over baked crust and bake another 25 minutes. Cool. For the topping, melt topping ingredients in top of double boiler. Spread over baked ingredients. Cool and cut into squares. Makes 3 dozen.

You'll think you're eating candy!

Almond Fudge Shortbread

2 sticks margarine, softened
1 cup powdered sugar
¼ teaspoon salt
1¼ cups flour
1 (12 ounce) package chocolate chips
1 (14 ounce) can sweetened condensed milk
½ teaspoon almond extract
1 (2½ ounce) package almonds, toasted

Preheat oven to 350 degrees. Grease a 9 x 13 inch baking pan. In mixer bowl, beat together the margarine, sugar and salt. Stir in flour. Pat into the prepared pan and bake for 15 minutes. In a medium saucepan, over low heat, melt chocolate chips with the sweetened condensed milk, stirring constantly until chips are melted. Stir in almond extract. Spread evenly over shortbread and sprinkle with almonds. Refrigerate several hours or until firm. Cut into bars. They may be stored at room temperature.

Million Dollar Bars

1 stick margarine
2 cups graham cracker crumbs
1 (6-ounce) package chocolate chips
1 (6-ounce) package butterscotch chips
1 cup chopped pecans
1 can coconut
1 can sweetened condensed milk

Melt margarine in bottom of a 9 x 13 inch pyrex baking dish. Sprinkle crumbs over margarine and stir. Add layers of chocolate chips, butterscotch chips, pecans and coconut. Pour the condensed milk over top and bake at 325 degrees for about 30 minutes. Cool in pan and cut into bars.

Carmelitas

Crust:
1 cup flour
¾ cup packed brown sugar
⅛ teaspoon salt
1 cup quick-cooking oats
½ teaspoon baking soda
1½ sticks margarine, melted

Filling:
1 (6 ounce) package chocolate chips
¾ cup chopped pecans
1 (12-ounce) jar caramel ice cream topping
3 tablespoons flour

Combine all crust ingredients together in a large mixing bowl, blending well with mixer to form crumbs. Press ⅔ of crumbs into a greased 9 x 13 inch baking pan. Bake at 350 degrees for 10 minutes. Remove from oven and sprinkle with chocolate chips and pecans. Blend caramel topping with flour and spread over chips and pecans. Sprinkle with remaining crumb mixture. Bake 20 minutes or until golden brown. Chill for 2 hours before cutting into squares.

Butter Pecan Turtle Bars

2 cups flour
¾ cup packed light brown sugar
1 stick margarine, softened
1½ cups pecans, lightly chopped
¾ cup packed light brown sugar
1⅓ sticks margarine
4 squares semi-sweet chocolate
½ stick margarine

In a large mixing bowl, combine flour, ¾ cup brown sugar and margarine and blend until crumbly. Pat firmly into a greased 9 x 13 baking pan. Sprinkle pecans over unbaked crust. Set aside. In a small saucepan, combine ¾ cup brown sugar and 1⅔ sticks margarine. Cook over medium heat, stirring constantly. When mixture comes to a boil, boil for 1 minute, stirring constantly. Drizzle this caramel sauce over pecans and crust. Bake at 350 degrees for 18 to 20 minutes or until caramel layer is bubbly. Remove from oven and cool. In a saucepan, melt chocolate squares and margarine and stir until smooth. Pour over bars and spread around. Cool and cut into bars.

Shortbread Crunchies

2 sticks margarine, softened
1 cup oil
1 cup sugar
1 cup packed brown sugar
1 egg
1 teaspoon vanilla
1 cup quick-cooking oats
3½ cups sifted flour
1 teaspoon baking soda
1 teaspoon salt
1 cup crushed Cornflakes
1 can coconut
1 cup chopped pecans

Cream together the margarine, oil and sugars; then add egg and vanilla and mix well. Add oats and dry ingredients and mix. Add the Cornflakes, coconut and pecans last and mix. Drop by teaspoon on an ungreased cookie sheet. Flatten with fork dipped in water. Bake at 325°for 15 minutes or until only slightly browned.

Melts in your mouth!

Glazed Butterscotch Brownies

3 cups packed brown sugar
2 sticks margarine, softened
3 eggs
3 cups flour
2 tablespoons baking powder
½ teaspoon salt
1½ cups chopped pecans
1 cup coconut

Glaze:
½ cup brown sugar, packed
⅓ cup evaporated milk
1 stick margarine
2 tablespoons baking powder
⅛ teaspoon salt
1 cup powdered sugar
½ teaspoon vanilla

Combine and beat sugar and margarine until fluffy; add eggs and blend. Sift flour, baking powder and salt together and add to the other mixture 1 cup at a time. Add pecans and coconut. Spread batter into a large 11 x 17 well greased pan and bake at 350 degrees for 20 to 25 minutes. (Batter will be hard to spread.) For glaze: In a saucepan, combine the brown sugar, milk, margarine and salt and bring to a boil. Cool slightly, and add powdered sugar and vanilla and beat until smooth. Spread over cooled brownies.

Cheerleaders' Brownies

²/₃ cup oil
2 cups sugar
¹/₃ cup Karo syrup
4 eggs, beaten
½ cup cocoa
1½ cups flour
½ teaspoon salt
1 teaspoon baking powder
2 teaspoons vanilla
1 cup chopped pecans

Beat together the oil, sugar, Karo syrup and eggs. Add cocoa, flour, salt, baking powder and vanilla. Beat well and add the pecans. Bake in a greased and floured 9 x 13 inch baking pan at 350 degrees for 45 minutes.

I baked so many pans of brownies the 4 years my daughter was in high school that I named them Cheerleader's Brownies-and I do believe those girls appreciated their "chocolate fix"!

Family Favorite Fudge

4½ cups sugar
1 (12 ounce) can evaporated milk
2 sticks margarine
3 (6 ounce) packages chocolate chips
1 tablespoon vanilla
1½ cups chopped pecans

Bring sugar and milk to a rolling boil that cannot be stirred down. Boil for exactly 6 minutes, stirring constantly. Remove from heat, add margarine and chocolate chips; stir until margarine and chips have melted. Add the vanilla and pecans; stir well. Pour into a buttered 9 x 13 inch dish; let stand at least 6 hours or overnight before cutting. Store in a tight container.

Macadamia Candy

2 (3 ounce) jars Macadamia nuts
1 (20 ounce) package white almond bark
¾ cup coconut

Heat a dry skillet over medium heat. Toast nuts until slightly golden. Set aside. In a double boiler, melt the 12 squares of white almond bark. (If you don't have a double boiler, just use a skillet to put the water in and place the white almond bark in a saucepan.) As soon as the almond bark is melted, pour in the Macadamia nuts and coconut. Stir well. Place a piece of waxed paper on a cookie sheet and pour the candy on the waxed paper; spread out. Refrigerate 30 minutes to set. Break into pieces to serve.

*This is good, good, good! How **easy** can it get?*

Date Nut Loaf Candy

6 cups sugar
1 (12 ounce) can evaporated milk
½ cup white corn syrup
2 sticks margarine
2 (8 ounce) boxes chopped dates
3 cups chopped pecans (or English walnuts)
1 tablespoon vanilla

In a large saucepan, cook the sugar, milk, corn syrup and margarine until it boils about 5 minutes, stirring constantly with a wooden spoon or plastic spoon so the mixture will not scorch. Add dates and cook until it forms a soft ball in a cup of cold water. Take candy off the heat and beat until it begins to get thick. Add the pecans and vanilla and stir until real thick. Then spoon it out on a wet cup towel to make a roll. This will make 2 rolls of candy. Let it stay wrapped until it is firm enough to slice.

Absolutely delicious! My good friend has made this for so many years, she just "dumped" the ingredients in without measuring! So she made up a special "batch" and actually measured everything — just for me!

Creamy Pralines

2¼ cups sugar

1 (3 ounce) can evaporated milk

½ cup white corn syrup

¼ teaspoon baking soda

½ stick margarine

1 teaspoon vanilla

2 cups pecans

In a double boiler, combine sugar, evaporated milk, corn syrup and baking soda. Cook, stirring constantly until balls are formed when dropped into a cup of cold water, or until it reaches the soft ball stage on a candy thermometer. This will take about 15 minutes. Remove from heat; add margarine, vanilla and pecans and beat until it is cool and stiff enough to keep its shape when dropped on wax paper.

INDEX

D

Please send _____ copies of *Mother's Recipes*

@ $16.95 (U.S.) each $_____

Postage and handling @ $3.50 each $_____

Texas residents add sales tax @ $1.23 each $_____

Boxes of 10, 20, 30, etc. available @ $12.50 per book $_____
(tax/postage included)
Wholesale and quantity discounts available TOTAL $_____

Check or Credit Card (Canada-credit card only)

Charge to my ☐ Master Card or Visa Card

account # _____

expiration date _____

signature _____

MAIL TO:
Cookbook Resources
541 Doubletree Drive
Highland Village, TX
75077
972-317-0245

Name_____

Address _____

City _____ State _____ Zip _____

Phone (day) _____ (night) _____

— —

Please send _____ copies of *Mother's Recipes*

@ $16.95 (U.S.) each $_____

Postage and handling @ $3.50 each $_____

Texas residents add sales tax @ $1.23 each $_____

Boxes of 10, 20, 30, etc. available @ $12.50 per book $_____
(tax/postage included)
Wholesale and quantity discounts available TOTAL $_____

Check or Credit Card (Canada-credit card only)

Charge to my ☐ Master Card or Visa Card

account # _____

expiration date _____

signature _____

MAIL TO:
Cookbook Resources
541 Doubletree Drive
Highland Village, TX
75077
972-317-0245

Name_____

Address _____

City _____ State _____ Zip _____

Phone (day) _____ (night) _____

Cookbooks Published by Cookbook Resources

Mother's Recipes
•
Recipe Keepsakes
•
Kitchen Keepsakes & More Kitchen Keepsakes
•
Cookin' With Will Rogers
•
Fresh Ideas For Vegetable Cooking
•
Homecoming
•
Mealtimes and Memories
•
Cookbook 25 Years
•
A+ In Cooking
•
Texas Longhorn Cookbook
•
Road Kill
•
Little Taste of Texas
•
Leaving Home

To order Pati Bannister's
signed/numbered prints, artist's proofs
and remarques, please call
New Masters Publishing
at 800-647-9578.